Poster Annual 1999

Poster Annual 1999

The International Annual of Poster Art
Das internationale Jahrbuch der Plakatkunst
Le répertoire international de l'art de l'affiche

Publisher and Creative Director: B. Martin Pedersen

Editors: Heinke Jenssen, April Heck
Assistant Editor: Chelsey Johnson

Art Director: Massimo Acanfora Graphic Designer: Dana Shimizu
Photographer: Alfredo Parraga

Published by Graphis Inc.

This book is dedicated to
the memory of Robin Rickabaugh,
1945-1998.

SAVE

Contents Inhalt Sommaire

Remarks: We extend our heartfelt thanks to contributors throughout the world who have made it possible to publish a wide and international spectrum of the best work in the field of design. Entry instructions for all Graphis Books may be requested from: **Graphis Inc.**, 141 Lexington Avenue, New York, NY 10016-8193 or visit our Web site, www.graphis.com

Anmerkungen: Unser Dank gilt den Einsendern aus aller Welt, die es uns durch ihre Beiträge ermöglicht haben, ein breites, internationales Spektrum der besten Arbeiten zu veröffentlichen. Teilnahmebedingungen für die Graphis-Bücher sind erhältlich bei: **Graphis Inc.**, 141 Lexington Avenue, New York, NY 10016-8193. Besuchen Sie uns im World Wide Web, www.graphis.com

Remerciements: Nous remercions les participants du monde entier qui ont rendu possible la publication de cet ouvrage offrant un panorama complet des meilleurs travaux. Les modalités d'inscription peuvent être obtenues auprès de: **Graphis Inc.**, 141 Lexington Avenue, New York, NY 10016-8193. Rendez-nous visite sur notre site web: www.graphis.com

Commentary **Kommentar** Commentaire

Corinna Rösner: Die Neue Sammlung
State Museum of Applied Arts, Munich

"Posters of the Russian Revolution," published in 1925, is the first poster-related entry in Die Neue Sammlung's first inventory list. Although only a book, it exemplified the collection's international orientation and its aim to collect contemporary avant garde. This was reinforced by other acquisitions in 1925, the year the State Museum of Applied Arts (Staatliches Museum für angewandte Kunst) was founded in Munich. That year Die Neue Sammlung purchased a set of English posters from the Baynard Press at the Paris Exposition Internationale des Arts Décoratifs et Industriels Modernes, where Germany was barred from participating. In 1926 a roll of Swiss posters was bought, with works by Hodler, Baumberger, Augusto Giacometti, Morach, and others. Both older and contemporary posters followed, from Denmark, France, Austria, Hungary, the Soviet Union and other European countries. German posters were of course also acquired, from T.T. Heine and Hohlwein to Lucian Bernhard and Jan Tschichold, to name a few. This progressive acquisitions policy led to the dismissal in 1934 of director Wolfgang von Wersin, subordination under the Bavarian National Museum, elimination of the purchasing budget, and finally to a complete shutdown in 1940. The suspicions of prominent Nazis were not aroused by posters per se, but rather by what they saw as evidence, reflected in the collection, of "Jewish store merchandise" derived from "cultural bolshevism." Despite this, the director at the time, Ortiwin Eberle, was able to launch an exhibition in 1938 entitled "The Poster,"

which was the first to show hundreds of such in a cross-section of the international collection. Half a century of poster art from throughout Europe was represented, which besides Toulouse-Lautrec, Cassandre, and others, also amazingly included many works whose style would certainly have been judged "degenerate" by National Socialists.

Die Neue Sammlung is not a poster museum, even though posters constitute one of the most important of its departments. Our poster collection should be seen in the context of the overall concept of the museum, which differs considerably, in a number of aspects, from older museums for applied arts. Unlike these other institutions, Die Neue Sammlung was founded in the early twentieth century rather than the nineteenth. It was set up between 1908 and 1913, reflecting the ideals of the Deutsche Werkbund, and became a state institution in 1925. The verve of the "Roaring Twenties" inspired its name Die Neue Sammlung ("the new collection"), like movements of those years, such as the new realism, new typography and new photography. This confident name reflected what was actually quite a new concept: collecting internationally rather than nationally and, especially, collecting what was "new" rather than old in style—objects of exemplary design within the applied arts of the respective period.

This approach led to more than just another temporal focus; it opened up many new areas of collecting, reflecting continuous change in a modern, industrialized society, which, like industrial design, were not considered by traditional museums of applied arts, even well into the 1980s. The most important criterion for inclusion in the collection was, and remains, quality of design. Contemporary acquisitions, and the posters in particular, have almost always been received as donations from the designer or the commissioner of the poster, in response to our request.

Objects from the nineteenth and early twentieth century were always chosen with a view to their relevance to the history of the modern age. Around 1960, for example, before the hippie movement kindled a boom in Art Nouveau, the collection was prescient enough to buy a large number of early French and Belgian posters by artists such as Chéret, Toulouse-Lautrec, Bonnard, Orazi, Steinlen, Mucha, Meunier and Cappiello. Apart from this, in the 1950s and '60s attention focused on contemporary designers from countries famous for their posters: France, England, Germany, and especially Switzerland. Then came Poland, Czechoslovakia, the U.S., etc., and international themes—film posters, for example, which in 1965 were shown at a much-talked-about exhibition, whose impact was felt long after.

In the 1980s and '90s this acquisitions policy continued, with greater drive and selectivity. First in the spotlight was the brilliant poster art of Japan since the 1960s, to which was dedicated a 1988 special exhibition. Other exhibitions and publications gave detailed attention to such subjects as merchandising posters (1981), posters by American and French artists after 1945 (1990/91), and travel posters (1995). There have also been shows dedicated to specific artists, such as Raymond Savignac (1982), Mendell & Oberer (1987)—who since 1980 have been responsible for the overall visual design of Die Neue Sammlung, including the award-winning exhibition posters—and Armin Hofmann (1989).

All these were examples of the classic definition of the poster as a "screaming picture," with clear, indisputably legible messages and functional typography. It was not until the 1990s that other, contradictory trends were recognized as worthy of inclusion in the collection: deconstruction, complexity, diverging motifs and typefaces, graphic variety, even distortion. Among such designers are Wolfgang Weingart, April Greiman, Gerd Dumbar, and the Grapus group, to name but a few. There are gaps in our collection, which hopefully can be filled.

Die Neue Sammlung responded to the radical revolution in style brought about by digital technology and new modes of perception by launching the very first exhibitions of David Carson (1995) and Tomato (1997). Significantly, these shows did not feature posters at all.

All museum people are aware that their work is necessarily selective. Die Neue Sammlung is no different, concentrating on carefully chosen examples: no collection can be complete. A comparison with poster collections of other internationally active institutions makes this particularly obvious—for example, the Hamburg Museum of Arts and Crafts, the Zurich Museum of Design, the Art Library in Berlin, or the poster museums of Wilanow and Lahti. There is no way we can measure up to these massive collections with our 15,000 or so posters in quantitative terms, but we can justifiably compare them in quality. Our collection, streamlined as it is, offers a very clear overview of the history of the poster in all its aspects, from its early days in 1900, when it was recognized as an independent design object, up to the present. And although the present is "fin de siècle," it is nothing like the last with its poster-mania, but rather a time in which "the end of print" has been declared, and with it the death of the poster. But this bit of history is not over yet. We shall see and collect what happens next.

Die Neue Sammlung, with its future-oriented approach, is and always has been very much a "work in progress," actually a "museum in progress," continuously changing, ever so slightly, to incorporate new aspects. Each new object acquired is mirrored against the objects collected before it, and changes their image as well. This kind of process keeps the museum from petrifying into a repository for lifeless things of the past.

The constraints of the provisional housing in which the collection has been kept since 1925 make it impossible for Die Neue Sammlung to show more than a tiny selection of its treasures in temporary exhibitions. But this too will soon change, when the new museum buildings are completed in Munich and Nuremberg.

Dr. Corinna Rösner *has been the assistant director of Die Neue Sammlung Museum at the State Museum of Applied Arts, Munich and curator of its Graphic Design Department since 1990. She studied art history, archaeology and anthropology at the University of Munich in Germany and since 1985 she has been working intensively with posters, which she sees as oscillating between the extremes of rigor and the imagination.*

Poster for the book
The Discovery of Kabuki," 1974
Design: Ikko Tanaka
Collection: Die Neue Sammlung
Photo: Komma, Munich

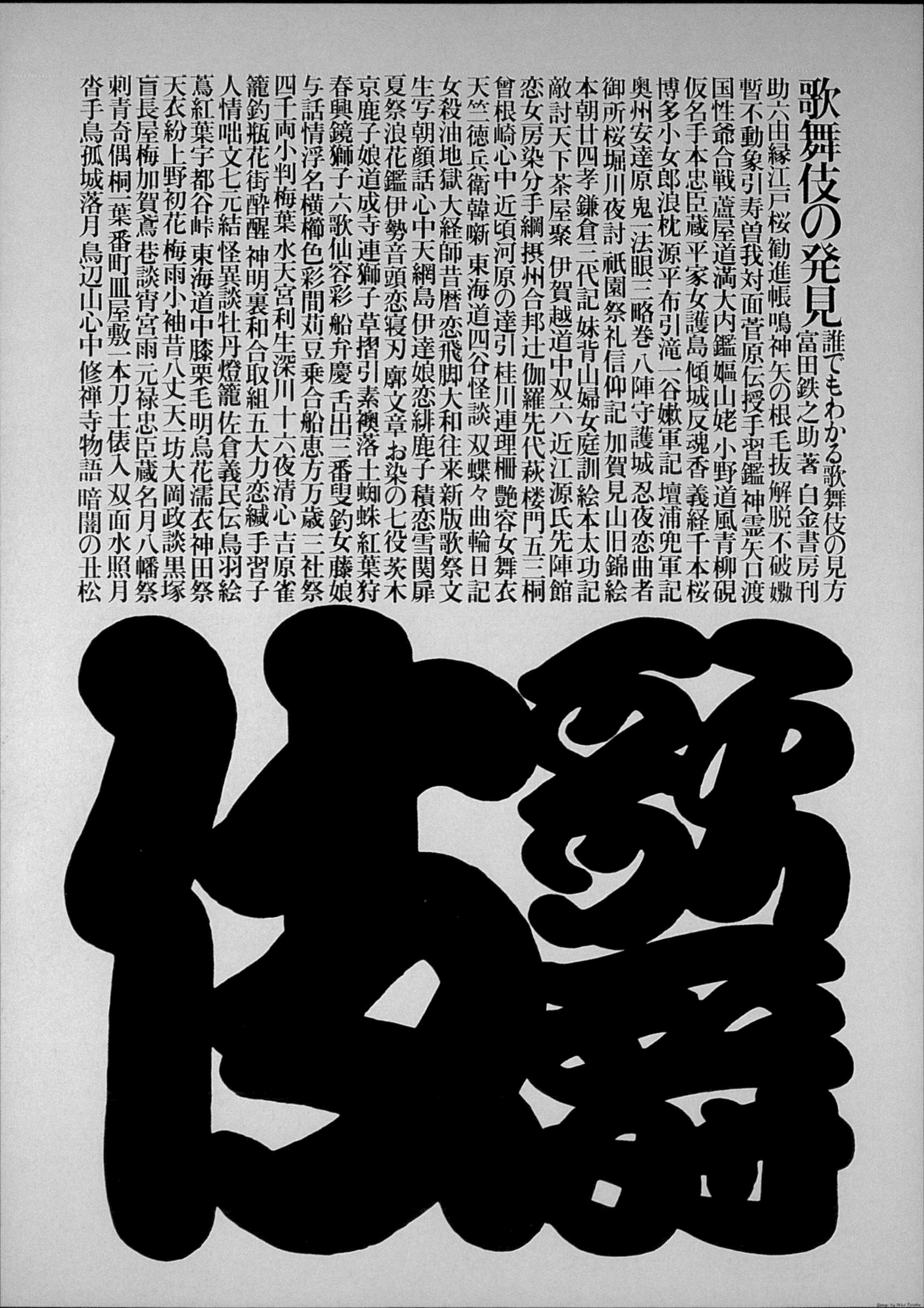

歌舞伎の発見 誰でもわかる歌舞伎の見方
富田鉄之助 著 白金書房刊
助六由縁江戸桜 勧進帳 鳴神 矢の根 毛抜 解脱 不破 嫐
暫 不動 象引 寿曽我対面 菅原伝授手習鑑 神霊矢口渡
国性爺合戦 蘆屋道満大内鑑 嫗山姥 小野道風青柳硯
仮名手本忠臣蔵 平家女護島 傾城反魂香 義経千本桜
博多小女郎浪枕 源平布引滝 一谷嫩軍記 壇浦兜軍記
奥州安達原 鬼一法眼三略巻 八陣守護城 忍夜恋曲者
御所桜堀川夜討 祇園祭礼信仰記 加賀見山旧錦絵
本朝廿四孝 鎌倉三代記 妹背山婦女庭訓 絵本太功記
敵討天下茶屋聚 伊賀越道中双六 近江源氏先陣館
恋女房染分手綱 摂州合邦辻 伽羅先代萩 楼門五三桐
曾根崎心中 近頃河原の達引 桂川連理柵 艶容女舞衣
天竺徳兵衛韓噺 東海道四谷怪談 双蝶々曲輪日記
女殺油地獄 大経師昔暦 恋飛脚大和往来 新版歌祭文
生写朝顔話 心中天網島 伊達娘恋緋鹿子 積恋雪関扉
夏祭浪花鑑 伊勢音頭恋寝刃 廓文章 お染の七役 茨木
京鹿子娘道成寺 連獅子 草摺引 素襖落 土蜘蛛 紅葉狩
春興鏡獅子 六歌仙容彩 船弁慶 舌出三番叟 釣女 藤娘
与話情浮名横櫛 色彩間苅豆 乗合船恵方万歳 三社祭
四千両小判梅葉 水天宮利生深川 十六夜清心 吉原雀
籠釣瓶花街酔醒 神明裏和合取組 五大力恋緘 手習子
人情咄文七元結 怪異談牡丹燈籠 佐倉義民伝 鳥羽絵
蔦紅葉宇都谷峠 東海道中膝栗毛 明烏花濡衣 神田祭
天衣紛上野初花 梅雨小袖昔八丈 天一坊大岡政談 黒塚
盲長屋梅加賀鳶 巷談宵宮雨 元禄忠臣蔵 名月八幡祭
刺青奇偶 桐一葉 番町皿屋敷 一本刀土俵入 双面水照月
沓手鳥孤城落月 鳥辺山心中 修禅寺物語 暗闇の丑松

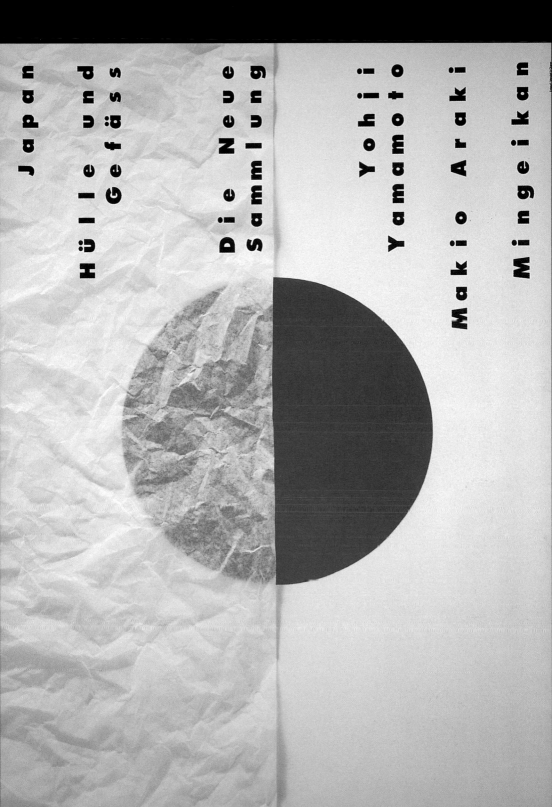

Japan

Hülle und Gefäss

Die Neue Sammlung

Yohji Yamamoto

Makio Araki

Mingeikan

25·11·92-2·2·93 Di-So 10-17 Uhr Staatliches Museum für angewandte Kunst Prinzregentenstr 3 München

Corinna Rösner: Die Neue Sammlung
Staatliches Museum für angewandte Kunst, München

«Das russische Revolutionsplakat», 1925 erschienen im Verlag der Sowjetunion, ist im ersten Inventarbuch der Neuen Sammlung der erste Eintrag zum Thema Plakat: «nur» ein Buch; trotzdem wird die internationale Ausrichtung ebenso deutlich wie das Ziel, zeitgenössische Avantgarde zu sammeln. Das belegen auch weitere Erwerbungen von 1925, dem Gründungsjahr dieses staatlichen Museums für angewandte Kunst in München. So kaufte Die Neue Sammlung auf der Pariser Exposition Internationale des Arts Décoratifs et Industriels Modernes, an der Deutschland nicht teilnehmen durfte, eine Gruppe englischer Plakate der Baynard Press. 1926 wurde ein Konvolut Schweizer Plakate erworben, darunter Arbeiten von Hodler, Baumberger, Augusto Giacometti, Morach usw. Es folgten frühere und zeitgenössische Plakate aus Dänemark, Frankreich, Österreich, Ungarn, der Sowjetunion und anderen europäischen Ländern, aber natürlich kamen auch deutsche Plakate ins Haus, von Th.Th. Heine über Hohlwein und Lucian Bernhard bis zu Jan Tschichold, um nur einige Protagonisten zu nennen.

Die progressive Erwerbungspolitik führte 1934 zur Absetzung des Direktors Wolfgang von Wersin, zur Unterordnung unter das Bayerische Nationalmuseum, Streichung des Ankaufsetats und endlich, 1940, zur völligen Schliessung. Das Misstrauen der NS-Prominenz entzündete sich jedoch nicht an Plakaten, sondern an den «jüdischen Warenhausprodukten», die, dem «Kulturbolschewismus» entsprossen, hier gesammelt wurden. Immerhin konnte der damalige Leiter Ortwin Eberle 1938 noch die Ausstellung «Das Plakat» durchführen, die erstmals einen viele hundert Beispiele umfassenden Querschnitt durch die internationalen Bestände bot, mithin «ein halbes Jahrhundert Plakatkunst» aus ganz Europa - und überraschenderweise finden sich hier neben Toulouse-Lautrec, Cassandre etc. zahlreiche Arbeiten, die als Werke «freier Kunst» sicher unter das Verdikt «entartet» gefallen wären!

Die Neue Sammlung ist kein Plakatmuseum, auch wenn der Bereich Plakate immer eine der bedeutendsten Abteilungen darstellte. Die Plakatbestände müssen daher im Zusammenhang mit der Gesamtkonzeption unseres Hauses betrachtet werden, das sich in wesentlichen Punkten von älteren Kunstgewerbemuseen unterscheidet. Im Gegensatz zu diesen wurde Die Neue Sammlung nicht im 19., sondern erst im frühen 20. Jahrhundert gegründet. 1908/13 in Verbindung mit Idealen des Deutschen Werkbundes begonnen, wurde sie 1925 als Staatsinstitution etabliert. Die Aufbruchstimmung der "Roaring Twenties" steht hinter der programmatischen Namengebung: Die Neue Sammlung, ähnlich wie die Neue Sachlichkeit, Neue Typographie, Neue Photographie jener Jahre. Der selbstbewusste Name signalisiert das grundsätzlich neuartige Konzept, nämlich nicht national, sondern international zu sammeln, und vor allem nicht die Stile der Vergangenheit, sondern «das Neue» zu sammeln - beispielhaft gestaltete Objekte der nützlichen Künste der jeweils unmittelbaren Gegenwart. Dieser Ansatz bedeutete nicht nur zeitlich ein anderes Gebiet, sondern auch - entsprechend dem Wandel der modernen Industriegesellschaften - eine Vielzahl an neuen Sammlungsfeldern, die in Kunstgewerbemuseen traditioneller Art - und zwar bis in die achtziger Jahre hinein - nicht berücksichtigt wurden, etwa das grosse Gebiet des Industrial Design. Oberstes Auswahlkriterium war und ist die gestalterische Qualität.

Die zeitgenössischen Erwerbungen und gerade auch die Plakate kommen seit eh und je meist als - erbetene - Donationen der Entwerfer oder Auftraggeber in die Sammlung. Retrospektiv ins 19., dann auch ins frühe 20. Jahrhundert zurückgegriffen wurde stets ganz dezidiert unter dem Aspekt der Entwicklungsgeschichte der Moderne. So wurden zum Beispiel um 1960 - glücklicherweise etliche Jahre vor dem Jugendstilboom der «Hippiezeit» - grössere Bestände aus der Frühzeit des französischen und belgischen Plakats erworben, darunter Chéret, Toulouse-Lautrec, Bonnard, Orazi, Steinlen, Mucha, Meunier, Cappiello.

Ansonsten galt die Aufmerksamkeit in den fünfziger bis siebziger Jahren den zeitgenössischen Entwerfern aus den klassischen Plakatländern Frankreich, England, Deutschland und vor allem der Schweiz. Dazu kamen Polen, die Tschechoslowakei, USA etc. und international übergreifende Themen wie zum Beispiel Filmplakate, denen 1965 eine viel beachtete, lang nachwirkende Ausstellung gewidmet wurde. Seit den achtziger Jahren wurde diese Erwerbungspolitik fortgesetzt - forcierter und stringenter. Der Blick richtete sich intensiv auf die überragende Plakatgraphik Japans seit den sechziger Jahren, 1988 in einer Ausstellung gewürdigt. Themen wie Warenplakate (1981), amerikanische und französische Künstlerplakate seit 1945 (1990/91) und Reiseplakate (1995) wurden in Ausstellungen und Publikationen erstmals konzentriert untersucht. Monographische Ausstellungen über Raymond Savignac (1982), Mendell & Oberer (1987) - die seit 1980 bis heute das gesamte visuelle Erscheinungsbild der Neuen Sammlung gestalten, also auch die vielfach preisgekrönten Ausstellungsplakate - und Armin Hofmann (1989) ergänzen das Spektrum.

Dies alles stand unter dem Vorzeichen jener berühmten klassischen Definition des Plakates als «schreiendes Bild» mit klar und eindeutig ablesbarer Aussage und funktionaler Typographie. Andere, gegensätzliche Tendenzen wurden erst in den neunziger Jahren als sammlungswürdig erkannt - Stichworte: Dekonstruktion, Komplexität, divergierende Motive und Schriften, graphischer Reichtum bis hin zum Vexierbildhaften ... dafür stehen Gestalter wie Wolfgang Weingart, April Greiman, Gerd Dumbar und die Gruppe Grapus, um nur einige zu nennen. Hier gibt es Lücken, die hoffentlich noch geschlossen werden können.

Dem radikalen stilistischen Umbruch durch die Digitaltechnologie und den veränderten Wahrnehmungsgewohnheiten

Dr. Corinna Rösner ist seit 1990 Stellvertretende Direktorin der Neuen Sammlung (Staatliches Museum für angewandte Kunst, München) und Kuratorin der dortigen Abteilung für Graphic Design. Sie studierte Kunstgeschichte, Archäologie und Ethnologie an der Universität München und befasst sich seit 1985 mit dem Phänomen Plakat, das für sie zwischen den Polen «Strenge» und «Phantasie» oszilliert.

trug Die Neue Sammlung Rechnung mit den jeweils ersten Ausstellungen über David Carson (1995) und Tomato (1997) - bezeichnenderweise sind Plakate hier nun kein Gestaltungsthema mehr.

Die Ausschnitthaftigkeit ihres Tuns ist wohl allen Museumsleuten bewusst. Die Neue Sammlung konzentriert sich auf sorgfältig ausgewählte Beispiele; Vollständigkeit wird in keinem Bereich angestrebt. Nichts zeigt das klarer als der Vergleich mit den Plakatsammlungen anderer international tätiger Institutionen, wie z.B. im Museum für Kunst und Gewerbe Hamburg oder im Museum für Gestaltung Zürich, in der Kunstbibliothek Staatliche Museen zu Berlin oder den Plakatmuseen von Wilanow und Lahti. Mit diesen riesigen Steinbrüchen an Material können sich unsere Bestände von ca. 15.000 Plakaten in quantitativer Hinsicht nicht messen - sehr wohl aber in qualitativer. Weitgehend frei von Schlacken, erlaubt der selektive Bestand, die Formgeschichte, besser gesagt: die Kunstgeschichte des Plakates, unter seinen verschiedensten Aspekten zu veranschaulichen: von der Frühzeit um 1900, als das Plakat als eigenständige

Gestaltungsaufgabe erkannt wurde, bis zur Gegenwart. Wobei diese jetzt wieder ein «Fin de Siècle» ist, aber keines mit einer Affichomanie wie im letzten Jahrhundert, sondern eine Zeit, in der man "the end of print" ausgerufen und den Tod des Plakates schon oft diagnostiziert hat. Aber die Geschichte ist nicht zu Ende. Man wird sehen, wie es weitergeht - und sammeln.

Anders formuliert: Die Neue Sammlung ist aufgrund ihrer zukunfts orientierten Konzeption seit eh und je eine Art "work in progress" - ein sich ständig leicht veränderndes, neue Aspekte hinzugewinnendes "museum in progress". Jedes neu erworbene Objekt steht vor dem Spiegel der bisher gesammelten Objekte und verändert auch deren Bild. Dieser Prozesscharakter bewahrt das Museum davor, zum Hort toter, vergangener Dinge zu erstarren.

Seit 1925 in einem schon lange viel zu engen Provisorium untergebracht, kann Die Neue Sammlung nur winzige Teile ihrer Schätze in temporären Ausstellungen zeigen. Dies wird sich ändern, wenn die derzeit entstehenden Museumsneubauten in München und Nürnberg eröffnet werden.

Corinna Rösner: Die Neue Sammlung
Musée national des Arts appliqués, Munich

Edité en Union soviétique en 1925, «L'Affiche de la Révolution russe» constitue le premier ouvrage consacré aux affiches figurant dans la bibliographie initiale de la Neue Sammlung. Ce n'est peut-être qu'un livre mais, à l'instar d'autres acquisitions datant de 1925, année de fondation du Musée national des Arts appliqués de Munich, il révèle à la fois l'orientation internationale de la collection et sa vocation, présenter des œuvres de l'avant-garde. En 1925 donc, la Neue Sammlung se porta acquéreur d'une série d'affiches anglaises des Presses Baynard à l'occasion de l'Exposition internationale des arts décoratifs et industriels modernes qui se tint à Paris et à laquelle l'Allemagne fut interdite de participation. En 1926, la collection s'enrichit d'affiches suisses réalisées par des artistes tels que Hodler, Baumberger, Augusto Giacometti ou encore Morach. Puis, des affiches plus anciennes et contemporaines vinrent élargir le cercle des pays représentés: Danemark, France, Autriche, Hongrie, Union soviétique et d'autres pays européens. L'Allemagne ne fut pas en reste grâce à des productions de Heine, de Hohlwein, de Bernhard et de Tschichold pour ne citer que quelques protagonistes. Cette politique d'acquisition progressiste conduisit en 1934 au renvoi du directeur Wolfgang von Wersin, à la subordination au Musée national de Bavière, au gel des acquisitions et, finalement, à la fermeture du musée en 1940. Ce ne furent pas tant les affiches, mais les objets utilitaires collectionnés par le musée - des «produits de masse des grands magasins juifs», des dérivés du «bolchevisme culturel» - qui éveillèrent la suspicion des pon-tes du national-socialisme. Malgré tout, le conservateur de l'époque Ortwin Eberle parvint à organiser en 1938 l'exposition «Das Plakat». Pour la première fois, des centaines d'affiches de la collection internationale offrirent un vaste tour d'horizon au public en retraçant notamment un demi-siècle d'histoire de l'affiche d'art en Europe. Etonnam-

ment, les visiteurs purent admirer, outre des productions de Toulouse-Lautrec, de Cassandre et de tant d'autres, des affiches dont le style aurait sans doute été taxé de «dégénéré» par les nationaux-socialistes! La Neue Sammlung n'est pas un musée de l'affiche, même si une place prépondérante a toujours été accordée à cette forme d'expression. La collection d'affiches doit être replacée dans son contexte général, différent en bien des points de celui d'autres musées plus anciens. La fondation de la Neue Sammlung, contrairement à de nombreux d'établissements similaires, ne remonte pas au XIXe mais au début du XXe siècle. Initiée de 1908 à 1913, elle reflétait alors les idéaux du Deutsche Werkbund (association allemande de créateurs et de fabricants engagés promouvant l'esthétique et la qualité) avant de devenir en 1925 une institution nationale. L'atmosphère des années folles caractérisée par un besoin de renouveau a inspiré le nom du musée, Die Neue Sammlung («La Nouvelle Collection»), à l'image du nouveau réalisme, de la nouvelle typographie et de la nouvelle photographie de ces années-là.

Cette désignation hardie signalait en outre un concept de base résolument novateur: collectionner à l'échelle internationale plutôt que nationale et s'intéresser à tout ce qui est «nouveau» plutôt qu'à des mouvements stylistiques anciens, soit des objets contemporains et utilitaires au design exemplaire. Cette approche n'impliquait pas uniquement la concentration sur un autre domaine de collection temporel, mais, face aux changements profonds opérés dans les sociétés industrielles, elle ouvrait la voie à des domaines de collection tout à fait nouveaux, tel le design industriel, qui n'étaient pas représentées dans les musées d'arts appliqués traditionnels et ce, jusque dans les années 1980. Le premier critère de sélection était et demeure la qualité conceptuelle.

Pour ce qui est des acquisitions contemporaines, les affiches en particulier, il s'agit le plus souvent de donations faites à notre demande par des designers ou les commanditaires des travaux. Au XIXe comme au début du XXe siècle, l'intérêt historique des œuvres prises dans le contexte évolutif des temps modernes a toujours guidé le choix des acquisitions. Ainsi, dans les années 60, bien avant que le mouvement hippie ne s'enflamme pour l'art nouveau, le musée fit l'acquisition de nombreuses œuvres des premiers affichistes français et belges, dont Chéret, Toulouse-Lautrec, Bonnard, Orazi, Steinlen, Mucha, Meunier et Cappiello. Dans les années 1950 et 1960, le musée acheta également des productions de l'époque provenant de pays traditionnellement connus pour leurs affichistes: la France, l'Angleterre, l'Allemagne et surtout la Suisse. A ces pays s'ajoutèrent, entre autres, la Pologne, la Tchécoslovaquie et les Etats-Unis et des thèmes internationaux comme les affiches de cinéma qui firent l'objet d'une exposition très remarquée en 1965.

Dans les années 1980 et 1990, la politique d'acquisition se fit encore plus intense et sélective. En 1988, une exposition consacrait les productions des affichistes japonais depuis les années 60, réputés pour la qualité graphique de leurs réalisations. D'autres expositions et publications se concentraient pour la première fois sur des thèmes spécifiques comme les affiches de marchandises (1981), les affiches d'artistes américains et français depuis 1945 (1990/1991) et les affiches touristiques (1995). Le musée a également présenté des expositions monographiques: Raymond Savignac (1982), Mendell & Oberer (1987) - responsables depuis les années 1980 de l'ensemble du programme d'identité visuelle de la Neue Sammlung, dont les affiches du musée couronnées à maintes reprises - et Armin Hofmann (1989).

Tous ces exemples illustrent la définition classique de l'affiche, à savoir celle d'une «image criante» complétée par un message clair et lisible ainsi qu'une typographie fonctionnelle. Ce n'est que dans les années 90 que d'autres tendances contradictoires suscitèrent l'intérêt du musée: déconstruction, complexité, motifs et caractères divergents, variété graphique et même distorsion. Parmi les artistes représentés figurent Wolfgang Weingart, April Greiman, Gerd Dumbar et le groupe Grapus pour n'en citer que quelques-uns. Certes, la collection présente des lacunes, mais le musée espère bien la compléter. La révolution stylistique engendrée par la technologie numérique et les nouveaux modes de perception a incité la Neue Sammlung à présenter en exclusivité les productions de David Carson (1995) et de Tomato (1997) - bien que ces artistes ne soient pas vraiment versés dans la création d'affiches.

Sélectionner des œuvres fait partie intégrante de la vie d'un musée, mais contrairement à d'autres institutions actives à l'échelle internationale comme le Musée des Arts et Métiers de Hambourg, le Musée des Arts décoratifs de Zurich, la Bibliothèque d'Art des Musées Nationaux à Berlin ou encore le Musée de l'Affiche de Lahti et celui de Wilanow, la Neue Sammlung n'aspire en aucun cas à présenter une collection aussi complète que possible; elle choisit avec le plus grand soin ses acquisitions. Sur le plan quantitatif, les quelque 15'000 affiches du musée ne peuvent rivaliser avec ces collections gigantesques, mais sur le plan qualitatif, elles n'ont rien à leur envier. Sélective et ciblée, la collection du musée retrace tous les aspects de l'histoire de l'affiche: de ses débuts dans les années 1900, époque où l'affiche était reconnue comme une discipline artistique à part entière, à nos jours. Et si aujourd'hui, nous traversons une nouvelle «fin de siècle», l'affiche ne suscite pas le même engouement qu'il y a cent ans; nombreux sont ceux qui ont annoncé la fin de l'imprimerie et, avec elle, la mort de l'affiche. Mais le fin mot de l'histoire n'a pas encore été dit et seul l'avenir nous dira comment l'affiche évoluera et de quoi seront faites les collections de demain.

En d'autres termes, la Neue Sammlung, avec son concept entièrement tourné vers l'avenir, peut être définie comme une «œuvre en progression constante» ou un «musée en progression constante» avec une porte toujours ouverte sur le changement. Chaque objet nouvellement acquis se reflète dans le miroir des objets collectionnés à ce jour et en modifie parallèlement l'image. Ce type de processus empêche que le musée ne se pétrifie, ne devienne un cimetière de reliques. Depuis 1925, seule une infime part des trésors de la Neue Sammlung a pu faire l'objet d'expositions temporaires en raisons des locaux «provisoires» trop exigus qui l'abritent. Mais cette situation ne saurait durer: les nouveaux musées en chantier à Munich et à Nürnberg ouvriront bientôt leurs portes.

*Depuis 1990, **Corinna Rösner** est directrice adjointe de la Neue Sammlung et conservatrice de la section Design graphique du Musée national des Arts appliqués de Munich. Elle a étudié l'histoire de l'art, l'archéologie et l'ethnologie à l'Université de Munich et s'intéresse depuis 1985 plus particulièrement au phénomène de l'affiche qui oscille à ses yeux entre deux extrêmes, à savoir la rigueur et l'imagination.*

Poster Annual 1999

Design Firm: Pentagram Design
Art Director, Designer:
Michael Gericke
Client: AIA New York Chapter

AMERICAN INSTITUTE OF ARCHITECTS NEW YORK CHAPTER HERITAGE BALL! NOVEMBER 19, 1998

HONORING LEWIS DAVIS, SAMUEL BRODY AND RICHARD RAVITCH PIERRE HOTEL, NEW YORK CITY

Design Firm: Pentagram Design
Art Director, Designer: John Klotnia
Client: ASA

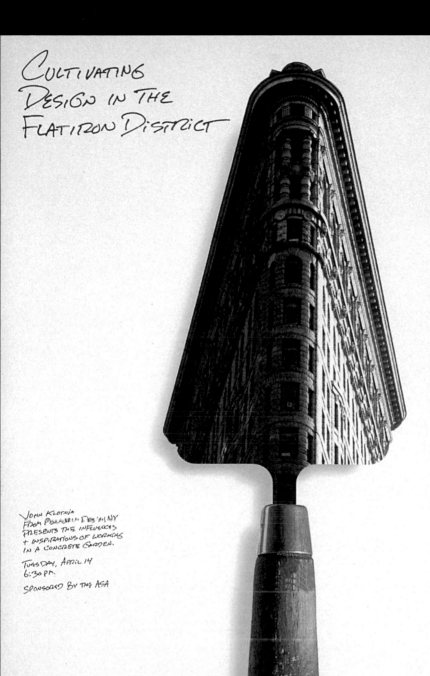

Cultivating
Design in the
Flatiron District

John Klotnia
From Pentagram Design NY
presents the influences
+ inspirations of working
in a concrete garden.

Tuesday, April 14
6:30 PM.

Sponsored by the ASA

Design Firm: Pentagram Design
Art Director, Designer:
Michael Gericke
Client: Skyscraper Museum

**BUILDING THE EMPIRE STATE BLASTING ALL CONSTRUCTION RECORDS & RISING
A STORY A DAY TO BECOME, FOR FORTY YEARS, THE WORLD'S TALLEST BUILDING
THE SKYSCRAPER MUSEUM, OPENING SUMMER 1998, 40 WALL STREET, NYC**

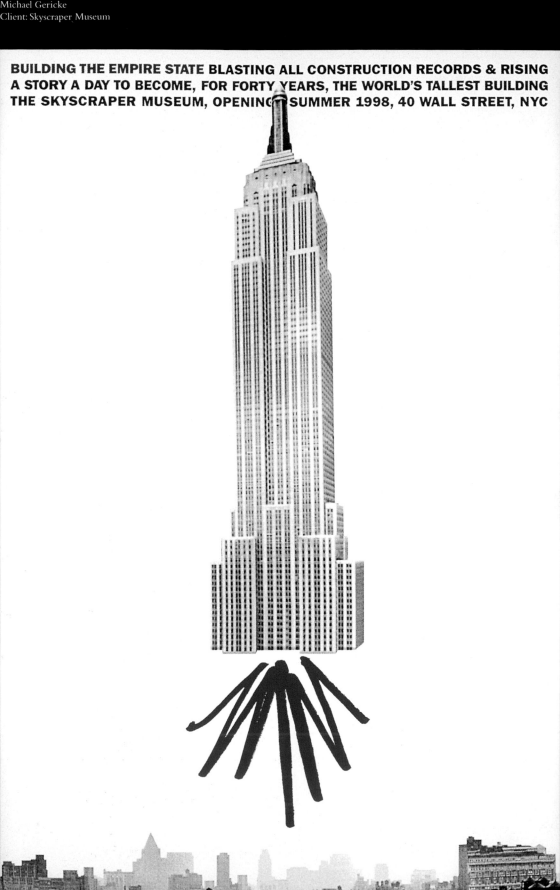

Art Directors, Designers:
Fons M. Hickmann, Christian Lessing
Photographer: Manos Meisen
Printer: Heerdter Lithopresse

"Exhibition and discussion on
the preservation of the public
house of studies"

Wollen Sie über kurz oder lang bezahlen?

278,-
Monatsrate

Sie können Ihre A-Klasse natürlich bar bezahlen oder bequem auf Raten. Zum Beispiel: Mit der Plus 3 Finanzierung der Mercedes-Benz Finanz GmbH sind es nur 278,- DM im Monat - bei einer Anzahlung von 30%, 36 Monaten Laufzeit, 7,9% effektivem Jahreszins und einer Schlußrate von 19.600,- DM. Fragen Sie Ihren Verkäufer nach den flexiblen Leasing- und Finanzierungsangeboten der Mercedes-Benz Lease Finanz. Oder wählen Sie unser interaktives Beratungssystem im Internet: http://www.mblf.de

Mercedes-Benz
Lease Finanz

Design Firm: Muller & Co.
Creative Director: John Muller
Art Director, Designer,
Illustrator: Mark Voss
Writer: Rob Holmes
Client: KPHN Radio

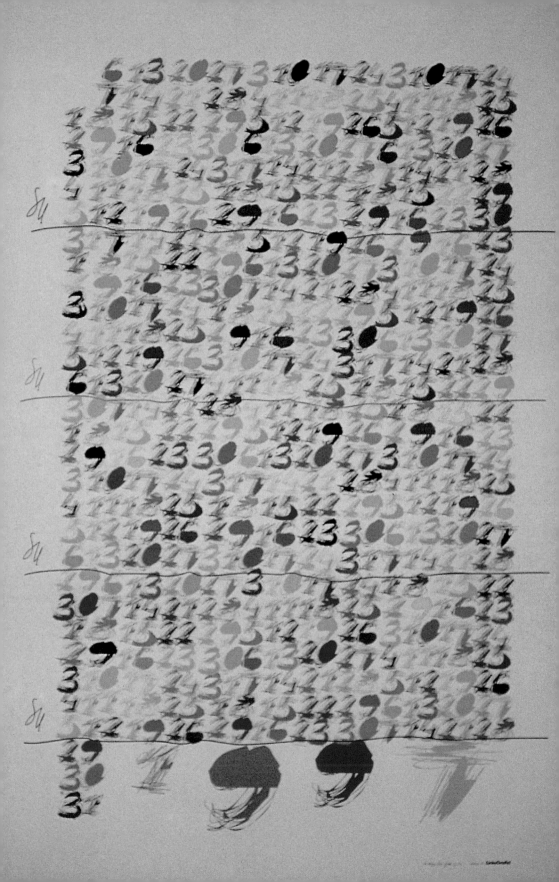

(opposite)
Design Firm: Graphis Zurich
Designer: Linia Grafic

(this page)
Design Firm:
Oden Marketing & Design
Creative Director: Bret Terwilleger
Art Director: Michael Guthrie
Designers: Billy Riley,
Vineet Thapar, Michael Guthrie
Photographer: Ben Fink
Writer: Rikki Boyce
Illustrators: Billy Riley, Michael Guthrie
Printer: Dawson
Client: Communigraphics
Call for Entries

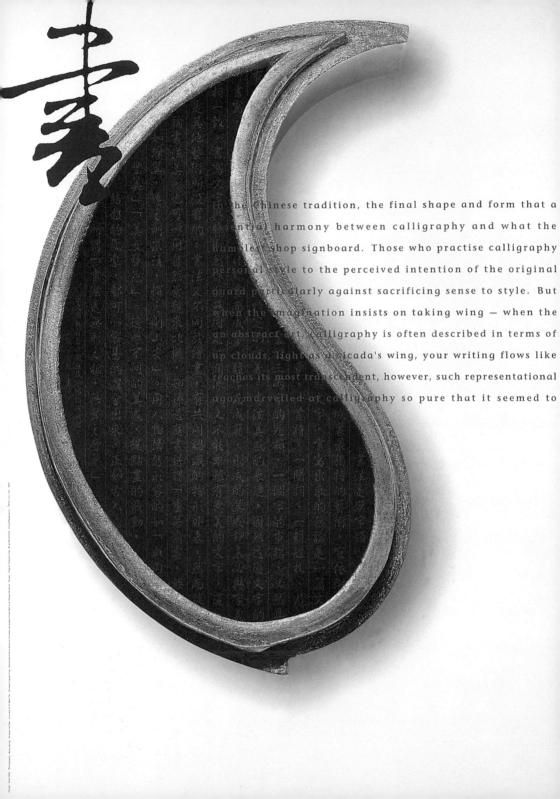

In the Chinese tradition, the final shape and form that a
essential harmony between calligraphy and what the
humble shop signboard. Those who practise calligraphy
personal style to the perceived intention of the original
guard particularly against sacrificing sense to style. But
when the imagination insists on taking wing — when the
an abstract art, calligraphy is often described in terms of
up clouds, light as a cicada's wing, your writing flows like
reaches its most transcendent, however, such representational
ago, marvelled at calligraphy so pure that it seemed to

writer brings to the characters in a message must always illuminate that message. An

characters mean runs through all forms of written expression, from the finest poetry to the

as an art form understand this harmony well, and they quickly learn to subordinate their

author. If they should decide from time to time to become their own authors, they must

if a regard for meaning is at the heart of Chinese calligraphy, there will always be times

brushstrokes seem to come alive with a unique message that transcends meaning. Although

nature imagery, as in Sun Kuo-t'ing's celebrated *A Manual of Calligraphy* "heavy as piled-

a stream, and ceases like a majestically serene mountain. When the calligrapher's art

imagery fails, and we can only fall back on the words of a scholar who, thousands of years

him like "... images without form, echoes that cannot be heard."

第10回
CSデザイン賞作品募集

募集期間＝1997年12月1日[月]──1998年3月31日[火]

［審査員］
永井一正（審査委員長）
田中一光
福田繁雄
菊竹清訓
内田 繁（新不可能植物）

［賞］
大賞 1点　副賞賞金 100万円
金賞 4点　副賞賞金 30万円
銀賞 4点　副賞賞金 20万円
銅賞 4点　副賞賞金 10万円

［後援団体］
日本グラフィックデザイナー協会
日本商環境設計家協会
日本サインデザイン協会
日本タイポグラフィ協会
全日本屋外広告業団体連合会
日本ディスプレイ業団体連合会
日本ディスプレイデザイン協会（順不同）

［協賛］
日経デザイン

［応募申し込み先とお問い合わせ先］
〒103 東京都中央区東日本橋3-7-13 相良ビル4F
株式会社中川ケミカル　第10回CSデザイン賞係
東京　　　03(3668)8141
大阪支店　06(543)2661
札幌営業所　011(736)4788
仙台営業所　022(271)9003
名古屋営業所　052(586)5681
福岡営業所　092(431)3013

主催　株式会社中川ケミカル

人間空間に色をさす

株式会社
中川ケミカル

(opposite)
Design Firm:
Nippon Design Center, Inc.
Creative Director, Art Director,
Designer: Kazumasa Nagai
Client: Nakagawa Chemical Inc.
Call for entry for "The 9th
Annual Design Contest"

(this page)
Design Firm: Skolos/Wedell
Creative Director,
Designer: Nancy Skolos
Photographer: Thomas Wedell
Client: Lyceum Fellowship
Committee

Design Firm: Dentsu Inc.
Creative Director: Yuli Tokudu
Designer: Hiroyuki Ito

Printer: Denta Tec. Inc.
Client: NTT

生きたネットワークへ。

NTT

小さなシステムも、大きなネットワークも

CUSTOMER-SIZING
by Team NTT

NTT

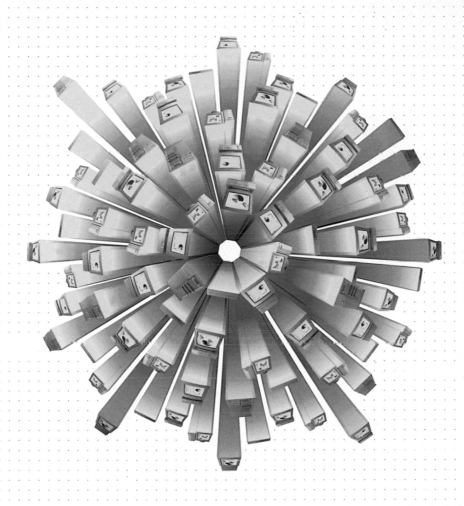

小さなシステムも、大きなネットワークも。

CUSTOMER-SIZING
by Team NTT

Enter

1996 South Australian Information Industries Awards for Excellence

premiere
content

nvidia corporation . experience it all.

IN

NVIDIA

(this spread)
Design Firm: Makoto Saito
Design Office Inc.
Art Director, Designer: Makoto Saito
Photographer: Kazumi Kurigami
Printer: Toppan Printing Co., Ltd.
Client: Masunaga Optical Mfg. Co., Ltd.

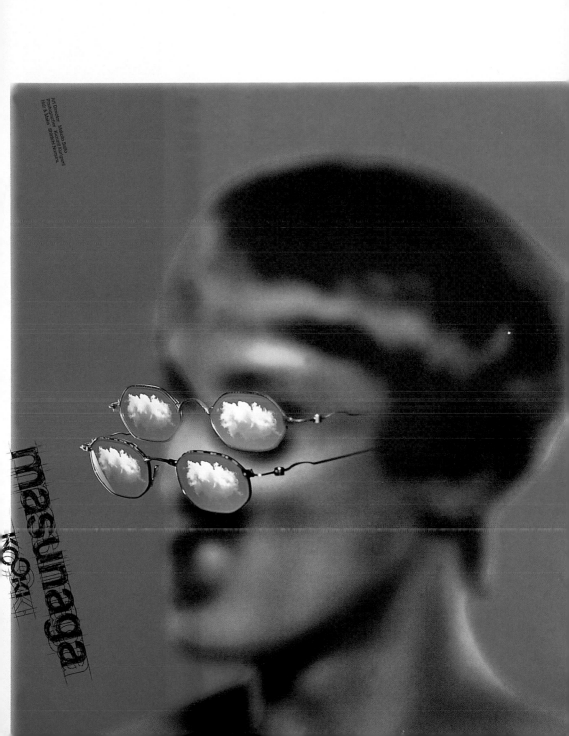

Art Director Makoto Saito
Photographer Kazumi Kurigami
Hair & Make Shiseido Norioka

masunaga

KOOKI

BUILD FOR
RETIREMENT. MANAGE
FOR LIFE.℠

Life is Good

You're lucky… and you're smart.
You've got dreams, and you
understand that dreams don't
come cheap. You're seizing your
opportunities, planning, and
looking ahead.

Because life is good, and it's
gonna get even better.

Ætna
Retirement Services℠

Netfinity
service
control
scalability
begin a new journey...
IBM

(opposite)
Design Firm: Desgrippes
Gobe & Associates
Art Director: Lori Yi
Designer: Joy Liu
Client: The IBM PC Co.

(this page)
Design Firm: Yokoo's Circus Co., Ltd.
Art Director, Designer: Tadanori Yokoo
Printer: Okabe Prints Editions Inc.
Client: Hikawa Shrine, Kawaguchi

(this page)
Design Firm: Qualcomm
Design Group
Creative Director: Chris Lee
Designers: Rudy Sabbagh, Adam Rowe
Writer: Crole Brummage
Client: Qualomm Inc.
CommunicAsia Trade Show, Singapore

(opposite)
Design Firm: Makoto Saito
Design Office Inc.
Creative Director: Ruki Matsumoto
Art Director, Designer,
Artist: Makoto Saito
Printer: Chuo Process Printing
Client: Ba-Tsu Co. Ltd.

(this page)
Design Firm: Packaging Create Inc.
Art Director, Designer:
Michiko Eguchi
Client: Tokyo Paper Mfg. Co., Ltd.

条件（g/m²）	81.4g/m²	104.7g/m²	127.9g/m²
四六判（1091×788mm）・Y目	70kg	90kg	110kg
包装枚数	200枚	200枚	200枚
菊判（939×636mm）・Y目	48.5kg	62.5kg	76.5kg
包装枚数	200枚	200枚	200枚
スノー	●	●	●
アイボリー	●	●	●

東京製紙株式会社

CANADIAN MESSE

はがきも直送い、やさしい質感
自然の色でマッチ、テクスチャで強くします

ラグジィアリィトな出版

文字も手の文、ネ力ログ、カレンダー、ポスターのほか
アニュアルレポートの本文に扱うページもなどなど
そんなとき性別を演出します

(this page)
(opposite)
Design Firm: Muller & Co.
Creative Director: John Muller
Art Director: Dave Swearingen
Designer: Jeff Miller
Writer: Pat Piper
Client: Alvin Ailey Ballet

(this spread)
Design Firm: Arrowstreet Graphic Design
Creative Director: Bob Lowe
Designer, this page: Ed Wonsek
Designer, opposite: Bob Lowe
Photographer, this page:
Lois Greenfield
Client: Chinatown Art Association

中國民族音樂歌舞晚會
An Evening of Chinese Music and Dance
A benefit concert to provide relief aid to the friends and families of flood victims in the homeland of China

John Hancock Hall　1998 年 8 月 29 日 (星期六)　8:00 pm　Boston China Art Association

華夏之夜

An Evening of Chinese Music and Dance

中國民族音樂歌舞晚會

主辦： 波士頓中國藝术家協會
波士頓華夏舞蹈團

sponsors: Boston China Art Association
Hua Xia Chinese Dance Group

協辦： 黃河藝术團
褚玲舞蹈學校
華姿舞蹈團

co-sponsors: Yellow River Art Society
Chu Ling Dance School
Hua Zi Dance Group

time: 8:00 pm, August 29, 1998
place: John Hancock Hall
tickets: $15, $20, $200 (honored seats)

John Hancock Hall   1998 年 8 月 29 日 (星期六) 8:00 pm

(opposite)
Design Firm: Slanting Rain
Graphic Design
Art Director, Designer, Illustrator:
R. P. Bissland
Client: Badly Bent Blues Band

平　面　设　计　在　中　国　9　6　展

主办机构:中华全国工商业联合会
深圳市科学技术协会
深圳市生产力促进中心
展览地点:深圳国际展览中心
展出日期:9月8日至11月8日

Organized by:National Industry and Commerce Union
ShenZhen Association of Science and Technology
ShenZhen Production Expansion Centre

(this page)
Design Firm:

(opposite)
Design Firm: Vaughn Wedeen Creative
Creative Director, Art Director:
Steve Wedeen
Designer: Pamela Chang
Illustrator: John Craig
Computer Production: Stan McCoy
Printer: Color Dynamics
Client: U.S. West
Poster for Internal Sales Promotion

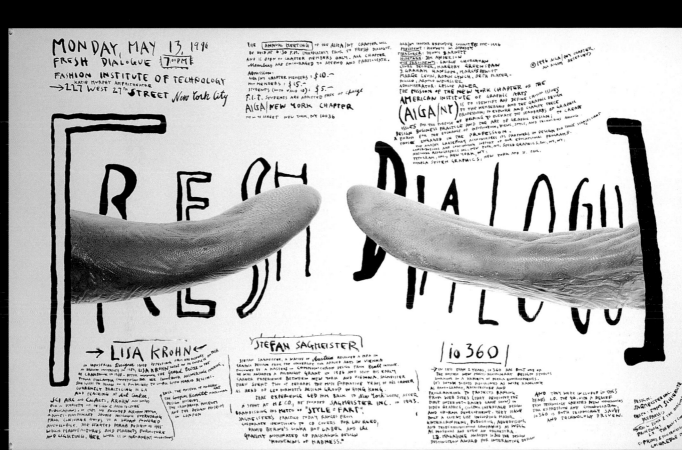

(opposite)
Design Firm: Dentsu Inc.
Creative Director: Yuli Tokudu
Designer: Yokoyama Fuminiro

Photographer: Takashi Seo
Posters provide information
for a private school

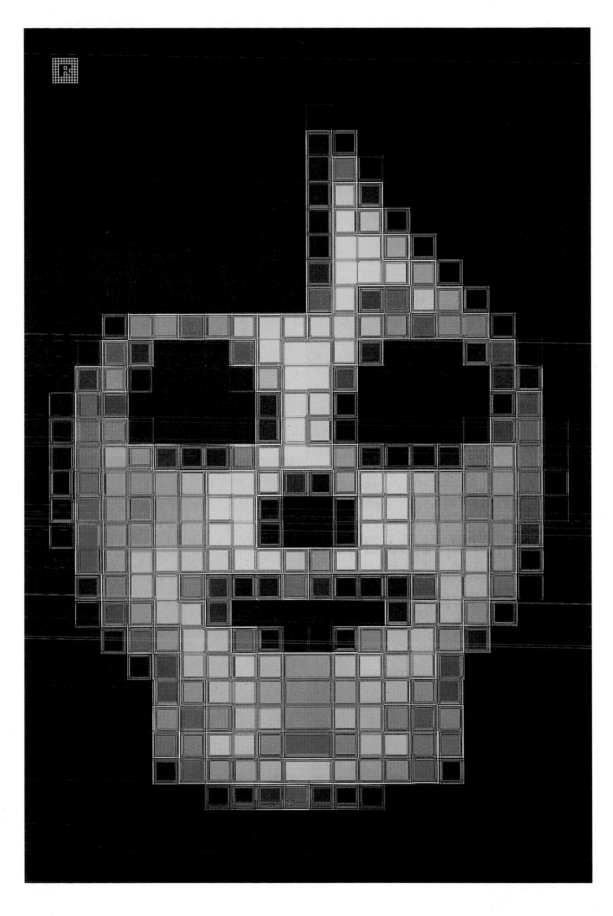

(this page)
Design Firm: Thirst
Creative Director, Designer:
Rick Valicenti

Printer: Brebner Printing
Client: Gilbert Paper
Gift for lecture attendees

(this spread)
Design Firm: Kan & Lau
Design Consultants
Creative Director, Designer:
KanTai-Keung

Photographer: C.K. Wong
Printer: G.L. Graphic Co. Ltd.
Client: DDD Gallery

YESTER**D**ATA

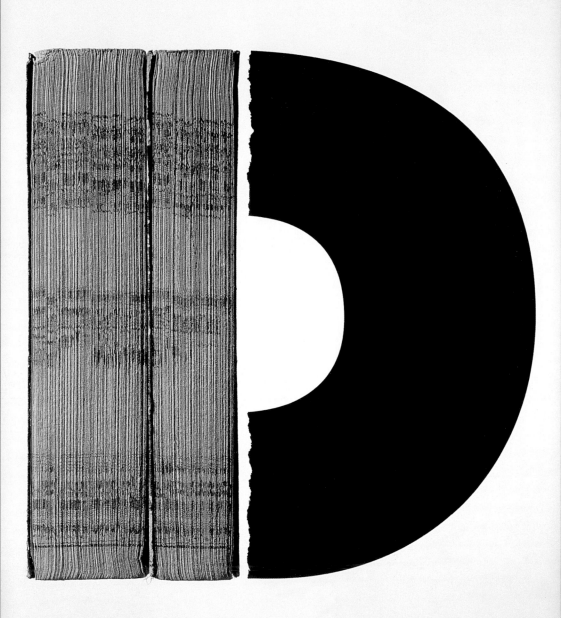

KAN TAI-KEUNG
HONG KONG · CHINA

PᵀAᴎᵀTᴲᴵᵀEᴎᵖᵀ

BRIDGE OF COMMUNICATION

(opposite)
Design Firm, Client: Kan & Lau
Design Consultants
Art Director, Designer: Freeman
Lau Siu Hong
Photographer: C.K.Wong
Self Promotion

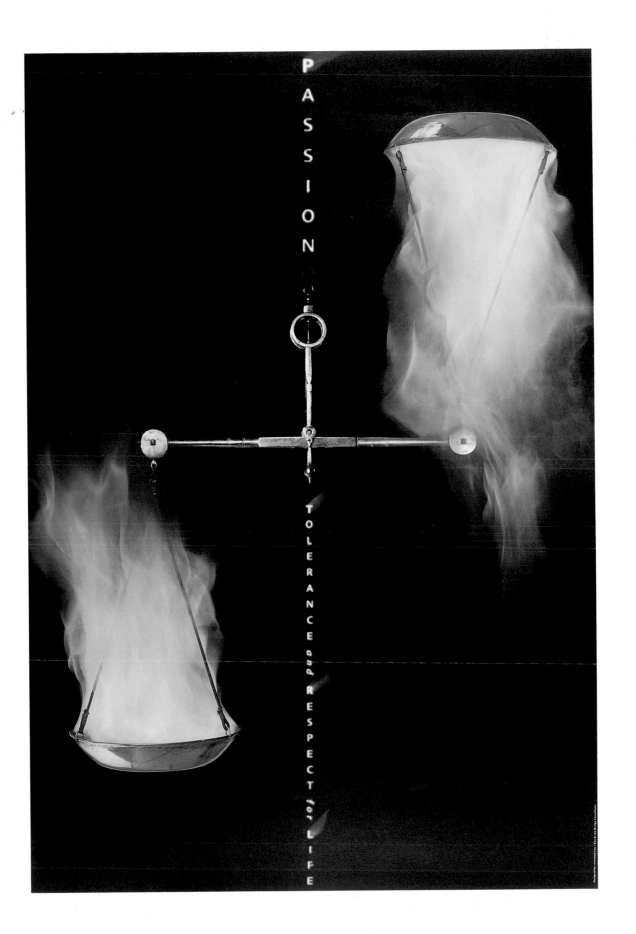

(this page)
Design Firm, Client:
John Brady Design Consultants
Creative Director: John Brady
Designer: Christine McIntyre
Photographer: Tom Gigliotti
Holiday Poster

CHRISTMAS
MEMORIES
FROM
JOHN BRADY
DESIGN
CONSULTANTS
PITTSBURGH, PENNSYLVANIA

Alan Chan Design Company
Hong Kong

Charles Anderson Design
Minneapolis

Koeweiden Postman Associates
Amsterdam

Mires Design
San Diego

Nike Design
Beaverton, Oregon

Pentagram Design
New York, London, San Francisco

Sandstrom Design
Portland, Oregon

Socio X
New York

Vanderbyle Design
San Francisco

VSA Partners
Chicago

ONE OUT OF TEN FOR ALAN CHAN DESIGN

Alan Chan Design, the only Asian design company selected as one of the world's top ten
for the year 1996 by Graphis Inc New York

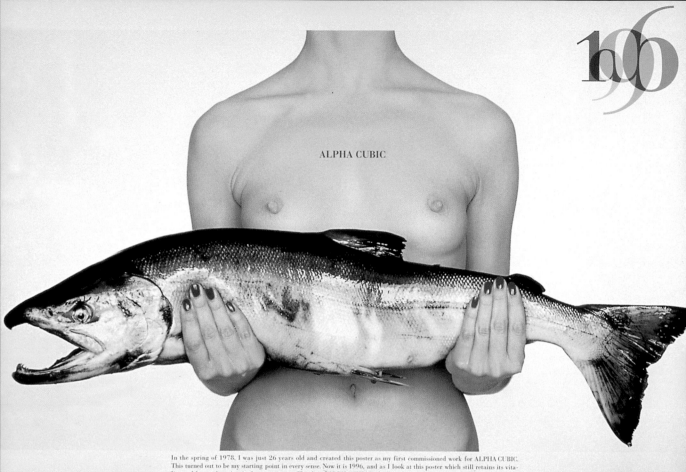

ALPHA CUBIC

In the spring of 1978, I was just 26 years old and created this poster as my first commissioned work for ALPHA CUBIC. This turned out to be my starting point in every sense. Now it is 1996, and as I look at this poster which still retains its vitality and luster, I am inspired to start anew. The client, ALPHA CUBIC, also has the same challenging spirit. / Makoto Saito

(opposite)
Design Firm, Client:
Design Bureau Agey Tomesh
Creative Director:
Arseni Mechtcheriakov
Designer: Dmitry Chernogayev
Photographer: Denis Kozyrev

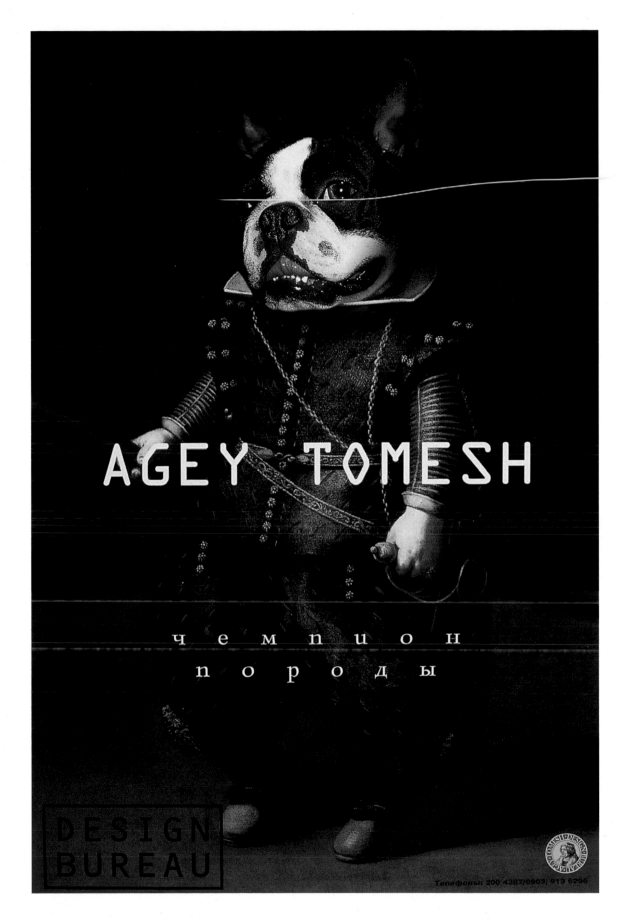

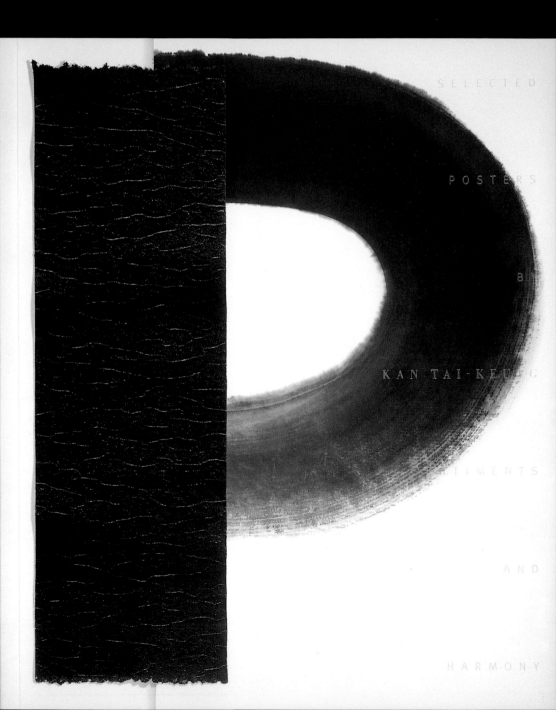

Design Consultants
Creative Director, Art Director,
Designer: Kan Tai-Keung
Photographer: C.K. Wong
Illustrator: Benson Kwan Tin Yau
Printer: Hong Kong Prime
Printing Co. Ltd.
Self-Promotion

SELECTED

POSTERS

B

KAN TAI-KEUNG

TIMENTS

AND

HARMONY

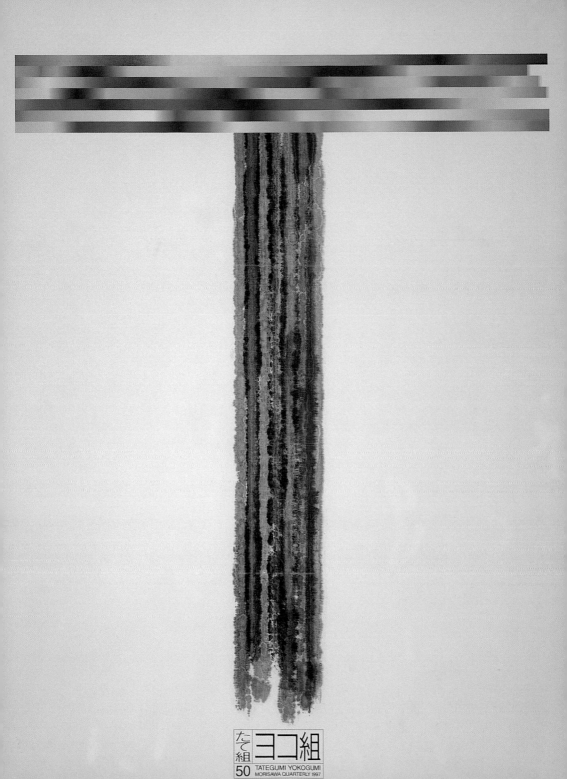

たて組 ヨコ組

50 TATEGUMI YOKOGUMI
MORISAWA QUARTERLY 1997

(this page)
Design Firm: BEK
Creative Director, Designer:
Bülent Erkmen
Photographer: Tülin Altilar

Printer: Ofset Printhouse
Client: Gutenberg Museum, Mainz
Exhibition poster for Bülent Erkmen,
"Works about Art and Culture"

Gutenberg-Museum Mainz
Liebfrauenplatz 5
22. Mai bis
3. August 1997

Öffnungszeiten:
Dienstag bis Samstag
10 bis 18 Uhr
Sonntag 10 bis 13 Uhr
Montags und an gesetzlichen
Feiertagen geschlossen

Sparkasse Mainz
DIE IDEEN-BANK

BÜLENT
ERKMEN
ARBEITEN
RUNDUM
KUNST u.
KULTUR

(opposite)
Design Firm: Sayles Graphic Design
Creative Director, Designer, Illustrator:
John Sayles
Client: Art Directors Clubs

JOHN SAYLES
SHEREE CLARK
SAYLES GRAPHIC DESIGN

ON THE TRAIL
TULSA
OKLAHOMA

NOVEMBER 20, 1997 TULSA GARDEN CENTER 2435 SOUTH PEORIA AVENUE
SOCIAL HOUR 6:30P.M. - PRESENTATION 7:30P.M. MEMBERS FREE
NON-MEMBER PROFESSIONALS $25 NON-MEMBER STUDENTS $10
ART DIRECTORS CLUB OF TULSA

100
KOKU
SCHOO
ANNIVERSARY

Design by Makoto Saito

100th ANNIVERSARY KOKURA TECHNICAL HIGH SCHOOL

ANNIVERSARY KOKURA TECHNICAL HIGH SCHOOL 100th

Design by Naruna Sano

san francisco
c a m p u s

new
building

CCAC's new san francisco campus will bridge the divides that

...Opens Fall 1996. CCAC's new san francisco campus will bridge the divides that separate art from technology from architecture from fine arts from design from each other. Opens Fall 1996.

illustration, furniture, illustration, fashion, graphic design, interior architectu...
...fashion, architecture, industrial design, graphic design, fu...

architecture in

& crafts california college of arts

(opposite)
Design Firm: Morla Design
Creative Director, Designer:
Jennifer Morla
Printer: Fong & Fong
Client: California College of
Arts and Crafts

School of VISUAL ARTS
Fifty Years

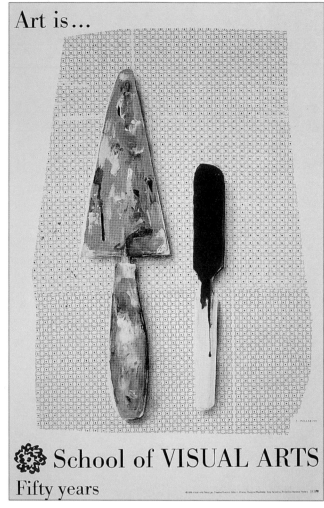

Art is...

School of VISUAL ARTS
Fifty years

ART
IS...

50th Anniversary
School of VISUAL ARTS

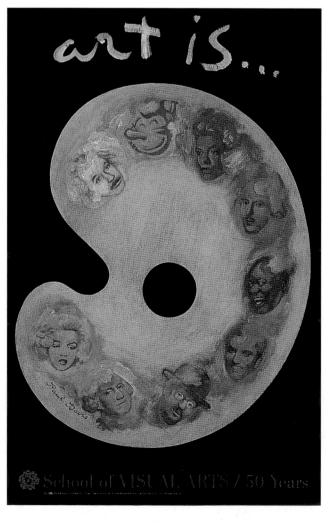

art is...

School of VISUAL ARTS / 50 Years

(opposite)
Design Firm: Visual Arts Press
Creative Director: Silas H. Rhodes
Printer: National Print Group Inc.
Client: School of Visual Arts
Subway posters celebrate SVA's
50th Anniversary

(top left)
Typographer: Kurt Houser
Collage and Painting: Marshall Arisman

(top right)
Designer, Illustrator:
Tony Palladino

(bottom left)
Designer, Illustrator:
James McMullan

(bottom right)
Designer, Illustrator:
Paul Davis

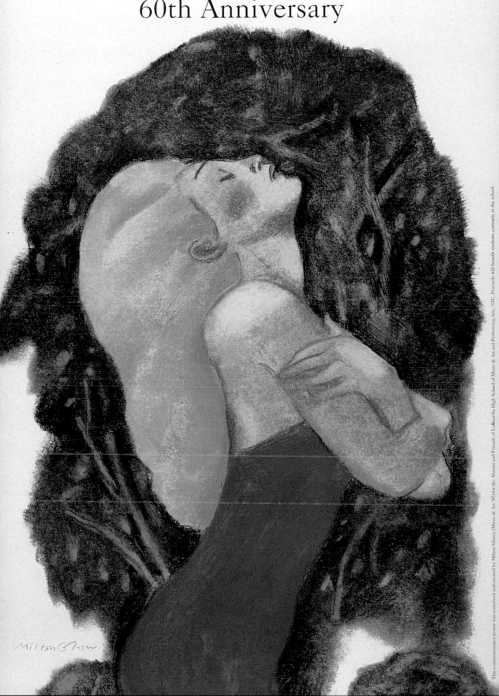

The art of teaching is only the art of awakening

The High School of Music and Art
60th Anniversary

(opposite)
Design Firm: Visual Arts Press
Creative Director: Silas H. Rhodes

(this page)
Design Firm: Milton Glaser Inc.
Creative Director,
Designer, Photographer: Milton Glaser
Client: LaGuardia High School of
Music & Art

(this page)
Creative Director, Designer:
Uwe Loesch
Client: Goethe-Instituts in France

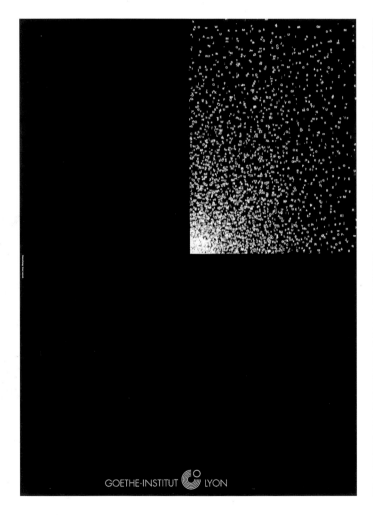 

(opposite)
Design Firm: Harold Burch Design
Creative Director, Designer:
Harold Burch
Photographers: Harold Burch,
John Senzer
Writers: Loretta Keane, Laura Mitchell
Printer: Presstime
Client: Fashion Institute of Technology

L E T H A L

So what's the catch?
Pollution is lethal.

Unfortunately pollution knows no boundaries. Pollution originating in the air, on the land, or the water is even on the other side of the world can eventually impact every living thing, including the fish that send us on our dinner plates, **and that's not red herring.**

Pollution prevention reduction of wastes at the source is the best way to reduce both point and non-point sources of pollution. Point source pollution includes industrial and manufacturing wastes. Non-point source pollution originates from automotive, construction agricultural runoff, and so forth.

National Pollution Prevention Week is celebrated every year to show off government agencies, private businesses, non-governmental organizations, and communities organizing various events and activities to put prevention first. President Clinton has proclaimed National P2 Week integral to the nation's environmental protection efforts.

Since 1995, the National Pollution Prevention Roundtable (NPPR) has promoted and coordinated pollution prevention (P2) activities across the U.S. NPPR also recognizes innovative P2 programs and events through its annual MVP2 awards.

So get off your pencil! For more information about NPPR, National Pollution Prevention Week and to find out how you can participate, call the official National Pollution Prevention Week Toll-free Hotline 1-888-P4-P2RO or check out the NPPR web site at www.es2.org.

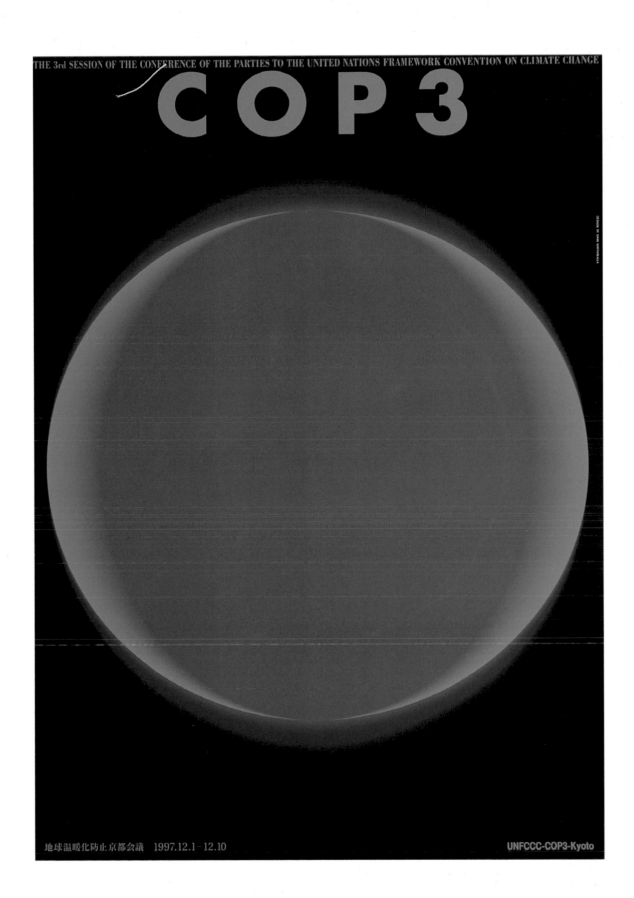

Design Firm: Packaging Create Inc.
Art Director, Designer: Akio Okumura
Printer: Ohtsuka Kohhan Printing
Client: Kyoto Committee for
Environmental Poster Design
Exhibition '97

earth

Let's talk before it's too late.

UNFCCC-COP3-Kyoto

earth

Let's act before it's too late.

(this page)
Design Firm: Sandstrom Design
Creative Director: Steve Sandstrom
Art Director: Amy Devletion
Photographer: Rick Schafer
Printer: Moore Litho
Client: SOLV

THE GREAT OREGON FALL '98
BEACH CLEANUP
SATURDAY, SEPTEMBER 26TH *from* 10:00AM *to* 1:00PM
FOR MORE INFORMATION, CALL SOLV *at* 1·800·322·3326
Come help keep Oregon's beaches clean and beautiful

(opposite)
Design Firm, Client: Looking
Art Director: John Clark, Rick Veda
Designer, Writer: John Clark
Printer: Gardner Lithograph

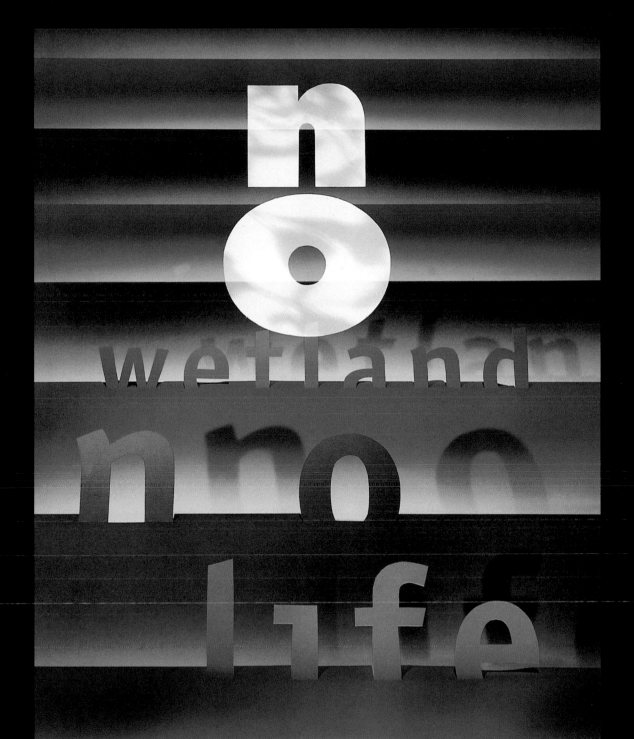

questions? call 1-877-4-wetlands

22.6.1994, klo 23.19

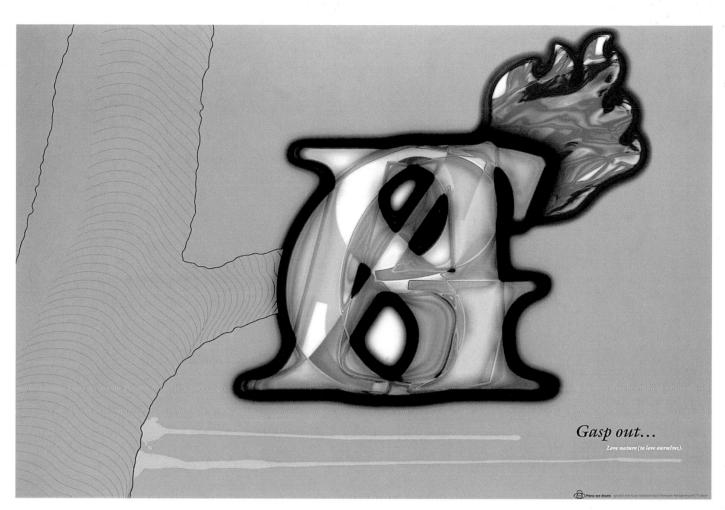

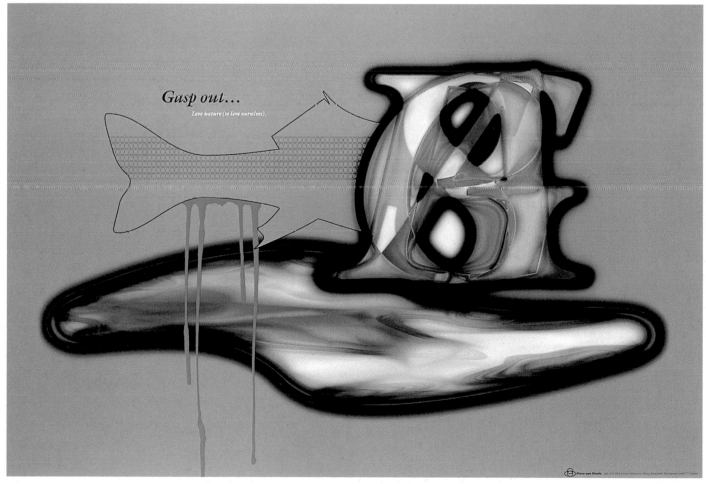

REGARDING USE OF PAPER
Reuse paper products to help reduce waste.

REPLENISH WHAT YOU TAKE

FROM NATURE, RENEW OUR

NATIONS FORESTS.

renew

replenish

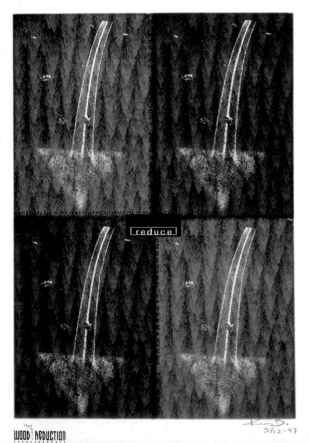

reduce

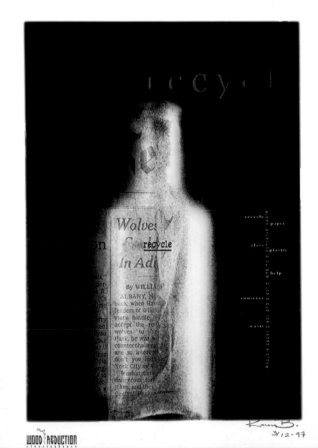

recycle

recycle

(this spread)
Design Firm: GK Design
Creative Director, Art Director,
Designer: Karen Brown

Photographer: Jaime Pandolpho
(Primo Angeli)
Printer: Urban Digital
Client: Wood Reduction Clearing House

REPLACE

FOR EVERY RING THERE'S AN ALTERNATIVE TO WOOD

Karen B.
3/12·97

Design Firm: Communication
Design 601 Bisang
Creative Director, Art Director,
Designer: Kum Jun Park
Photographer: Hoo Man Park
Illustrator: Wan Gue Lee
Writer: Joon Young Bae
Printer: Hong Il Printing Co.
Client: Ministry of Environment

Nature, that's the way to go.

Designer: Dawn Droskoski
Photographer: Schulz
Illustrator: Terry Oakes Bourret
Printer: Allied
Client: Durham Fair Association

The Durham Fair

The Seventy-Seventh
Annual Durham Fair

Connecticut's Largest
Agricultural Exhibition

September 27, 28, 29
Nineteen Ninety-Six

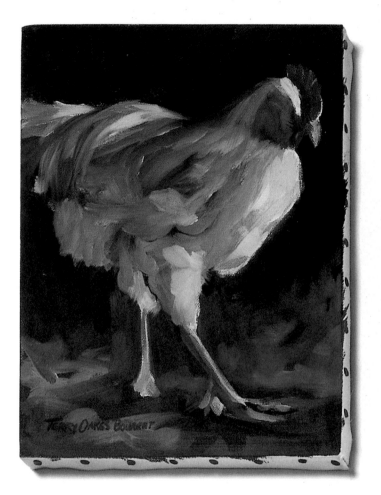

When tillage begins. other arts follow.
The farmers. therefore are the founders
of human civilization.

(opposite)
Design Firm: Ted Bertz
Graphic Design Inc.
Creative Director, Writer Ted Bertz
Designers: Ted Bertz,
Mark Terranova
Photographer: Glen Curtis,
John Giammatteo
Client: Durham Fair Association

Design Firm: Communication
Design 601 Bisang
Creative Director, Art Director,
Designer: Kum Jun Park
Illustrator: Jung Hye Suck

Writer: Joon Young Bae
Printer: Shin Won Printing Co.
Client: Visual Information Design
Association of Korea

Design Firm:
Ted Bertz Graphic Design Inc.
Creative Director: Ted Bertz
Designer: Dawn Droskoski
Photographer: Schulz
Illustrator: Terry Oakes Bourret
Printer: Allied
Client: Durham Fair Association

The Durham Fair

The Seventy-Seventh
Annual Durham Fair

Connecticut's Largest
Agricultural Exhibition

September 27, 28, 29
Nineteen Ninety-Six

When tillage begins, other arts follow.
The farmers, therefore are the founders
of human civilization.

Daniel Webster Platt

(opposite)
Design Firm: Ted Bertz
Graphic Design Inc.
Creative Director, Writer Ted Bertz
Designers: Ted Bertz,
Mark Terranova
Photographer: Glen Curtis,
John Giammatteo
Client: Durham Fair Association

Durham Fair 1997

The Seventy-Eighth
Annual Durham Fair

Connecticut's Largest
Agricultural Exhibition

September 26, 27, & 28,
Nineteen Ninety-Seven

The antique tool
collection at the
Durham Fair is
our connection with
our farming past.

Our great grandfathers'
harnesses and
clanging hammers
can still be seen,
touched and heard.

Art Director, Designer:
Yoshimaru Takahashi
Photographer: Koichi Okuwaki
Writer: Kenjiro Hagiwara
Client: Jyoka

(opposite)
Design Firm: Michael Schwab Studio
Art Director: Melanie Brooks
Printer: B & R Screen Graphics
Client: Polo Retail Corporation

FOR THE CHILDREN'S HOME SOCIETY OF MINNESOTA
POLO RALPH LAUREN AT YOUNG QUINLAN

PRESENTS

THE NINTH ANNUAL

POLO
CLASSIC

SUNDAY AUGUST 2, 1998

SCHWAB

(this page)
Design Firm: Wilson Communications
Designer: Joe Goodwin
Photographer: James Russell

Writer: Joe Goodwin
Printer: Heritage Press
Client: Dallas Society of Visual
Communications

(opposite)
Design Firm: Iconix Group
Designer: Rob Coleman
Photographer: Anthon Beeke

Printer: PSB Imaging
Client: F. Parsons Paper Co.
Promotion for lecture by controversial
Dutch designer Anton Beeke

AN EVENING WITH ANTHON BEEKE **THE NAUGHTY BOY** OF DUTCH GRAPHIC DESIGN

THURSDAY
OCTOBER 8
5:30 PM–9:30 PM

EMBASSY HOUSE
FEDERAL REPUBLIC
OF GERMANY

(this page)
Design Firm: Cyclone
Designers, Illustrators:
Dennis Clouse, Traci Daberko
Printer: Hemlock Printers Inc.
Client: AIGA/Seattle

(opposite)
Design Firm: Sommese Design
Creative Director, Writer: Steve Perry
Art Directors: Lanny Sommese,
Kristin Sommese

Designers: Steve Perry,
Kristin Sommese
Illustrator: Lanny Sommese
Client: AIGA, Philadelphia Chapter

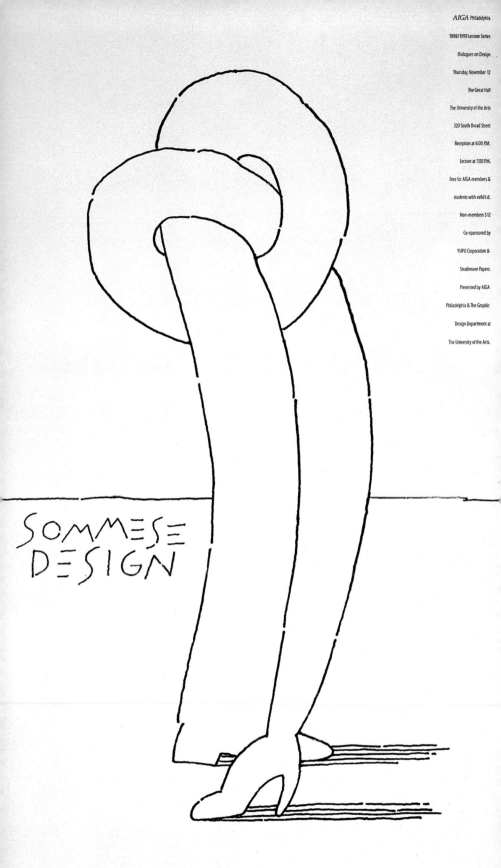

AIGA Philadelphia

1998/1999 Lecture Series

Dialogues on Design

Thursday, November 12

The Great Hall

The University of the Arts

320 South Broad Street

Reception at 6:00 P.M.

Lecture at 7:00 P.M.

Free for AIGA members &

students with valid i.d.

Non-members $12

Co-sponsored by

YUPO Corporation &

Strathmore Papers.

Presented by AIGA

Philadelphia & The Graphic

Design Department at

The University of the Arts.

SOMMESE
DESIGN

(this page)
Design Firm: Milton Glaser Inc.
Designer: Milton Glaser
Client: Art Director's Club

You are cordially invited to the 1997 Hall of Fame Dinner and Presentation

Honoring laureates Allan Beaver, Sheila Metzner, B. Martin Pedersen, George Tscherny

Thursday, November 6, 1997 at six o'clock in the evening

The Art Directors Club 250 Park Avenue South at 20th Street New York City 212.674.0500 fax 212.460.8506

Black tie. RSVP early as seating is limited. Reply card enclosed.

Special thanks to Color by Pergament for initial sponsorship of the Hall of Fame Video Project. This year's Hall of Fame presentation is being made possible in part by Daniels Printing, New York. Design by Milton Glaser. Paper by Mohawk.

(opposite)
Design Firm: Shima Design Office Inc.
Creative Director, Art Director,
Designer: Takahiro Shima
Printer: Toppan Printing Co. Ltd.
Client: Osaka Chamber of Commerce
& Industry/Osaka 21st Century
Association

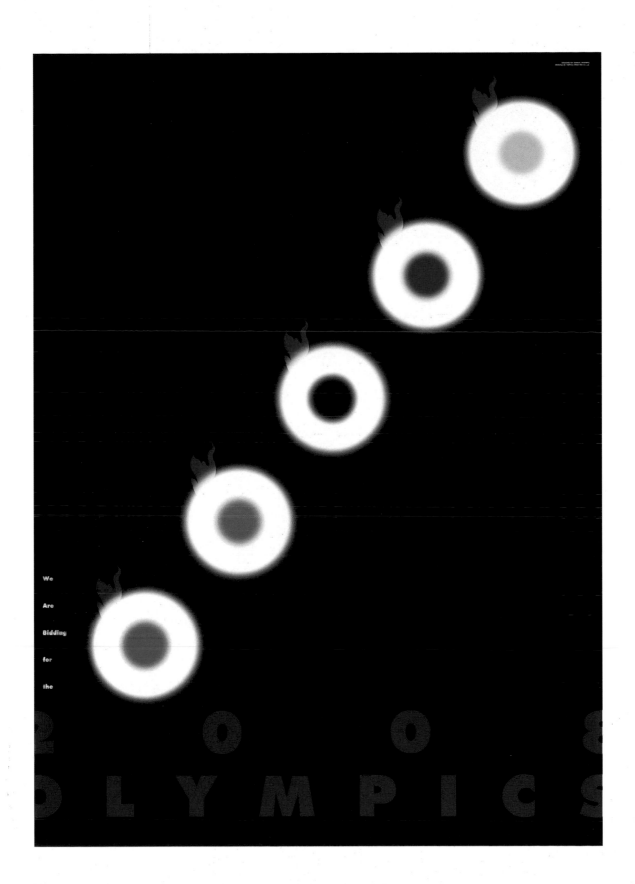

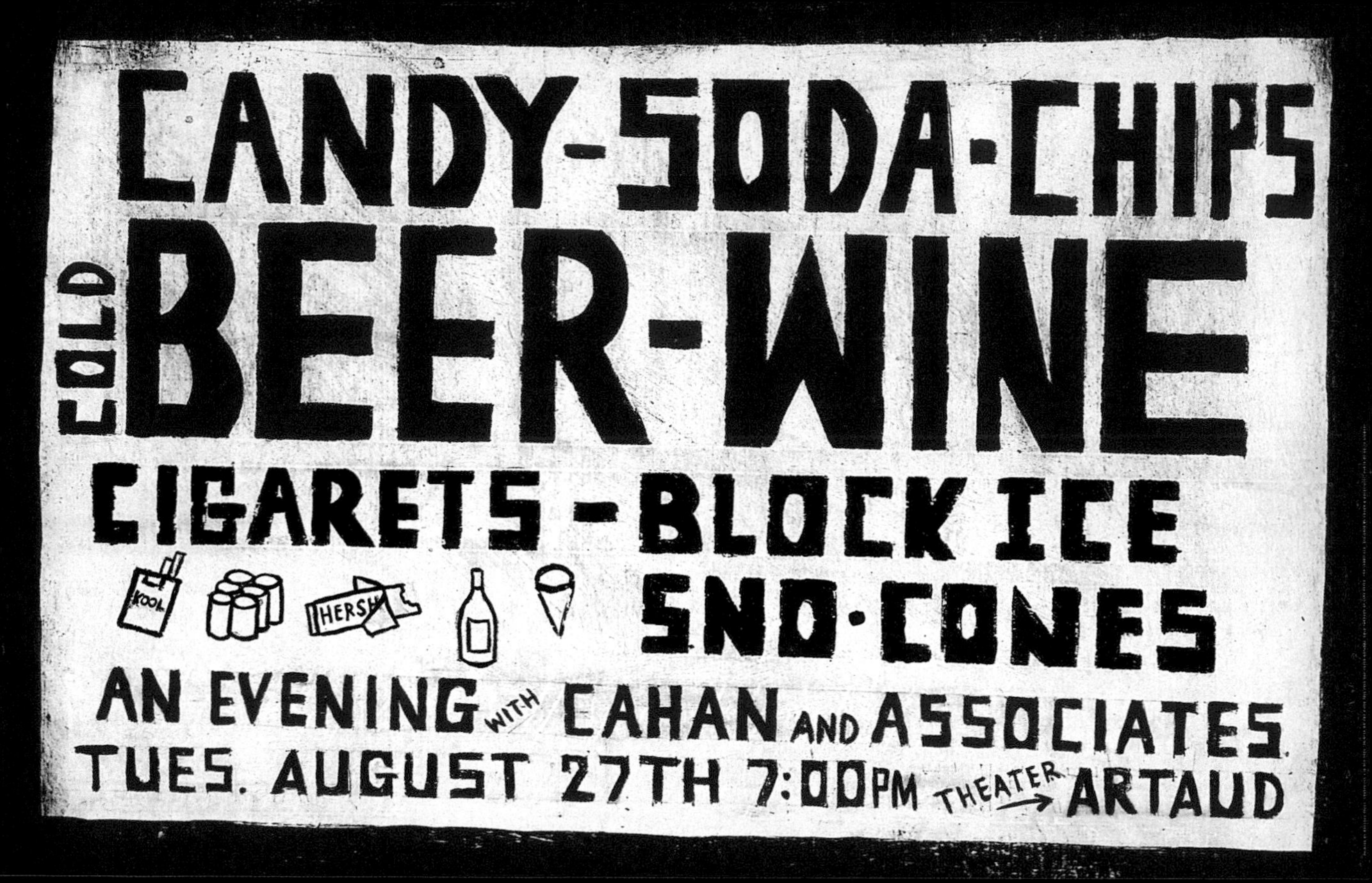

(opposite)
Design Firm:
Douglas Oliver Design Office
Art Director, Designer:
Deanna Kuhlmann-Leaviti
Photographer: Gregg Goldman
Printer: Lithographix
Client: Mead Coated Paper
Call for entry

visibility

going the distance. in it's 42nd year, the mead annual report show once again celebrates design and it's impact on the highly regarded, multi-billion dollar annual report industry. the mead show: bringing the annual report into focus

42

(this page)
Designer: H. C. Jenssen
Client: Stadtbibliothek Wiesbaden
Promotion for Literature Days
and an Exhibition

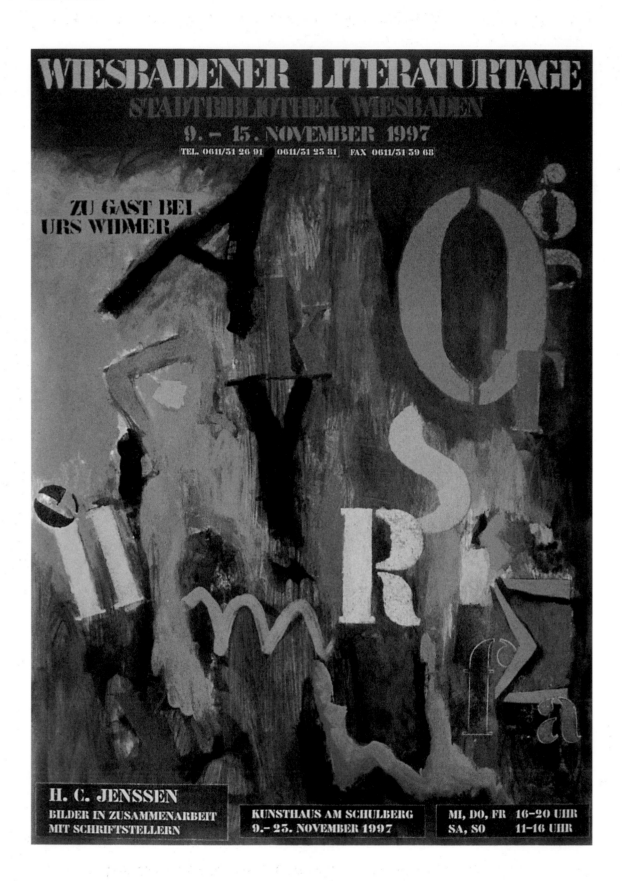

(this page)

(opposite)
Design Firm: Chermayeff
& Geismar Inc.
Illustrator: Ivan Chermayeff
Client: University of California
Los Angeles

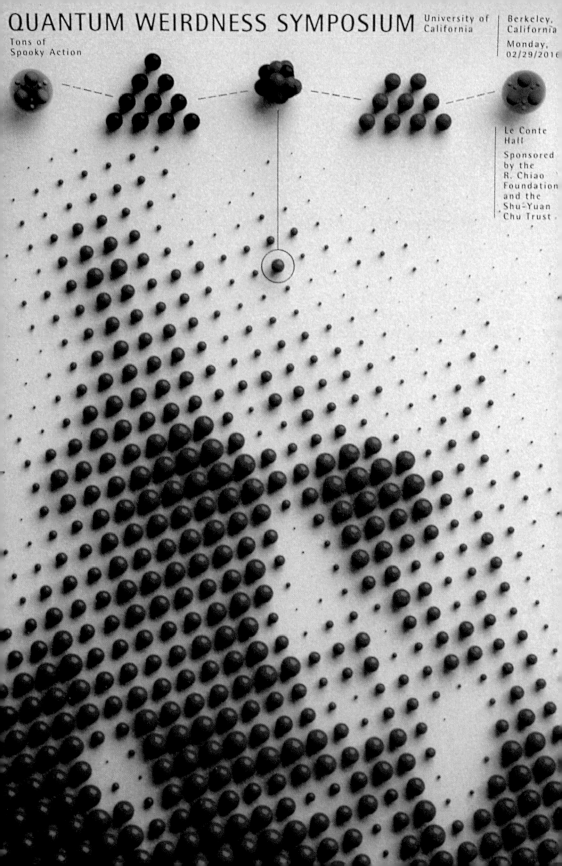

QUANTUM WEIRDNESS SYMPOSIUM

University of California

Tons of
Spooky Action

Berkeley,
California

Monday,
02/29/2016

Le Conte
Hall

Sponsored
by the
R. Chiao
Foundation
and the
Shu-Yuan
Chu Trust

(opposite)
Design Firm: Sagmeister Inc.
Creative Director,
Designers: Stefan Sagmeister,
Veronica Oh
Digital: John Kahrs
Client: New York Times

the second annual insect collector's convention of southern california

los angeles county aboretum
1356 baldwin avenue
arcadia california
december 20 & 21

(this page)
Design Firm: Aki
Creative Director: Michael Warrick

WORKS FROM
95/96
ÇALIŞMALARI

BÜLENT ERKMEN

23 ŞUBAT - 28 MART 1998
KABATAŞ KÜLTÜR MERKEZİ
B BLOK SERGİ SALONU
ORTAKÖY İSTANBUL

(opposite)
Design Firm, Client: BEK
Creative Director, Designer:
Bülent Erkmen
Photographer: Fethi Izan
Printer: Ofset Printhouse
One of series of posters for
biennial solo exhibitions

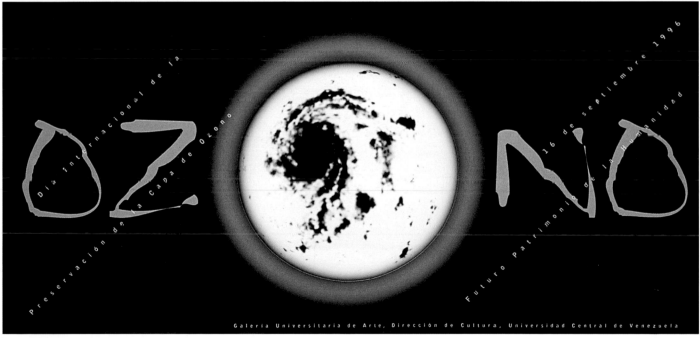

(this page)
Design Firm: Pontificia
Universidad Católica
Art Director, Designer:
Ximena Ulibarri
Client: Universidad Central
de Venezuela

THE *Benefit* *Cup*

AT *Rush Creek*

1 9 9 7

MONDAY

JULY

A CHARITY GOLF TOURNAMENT
BENEFITING PARTNERS IN POSITIVE PARENTING

PRESENTED BY
THE ASSOCIATION OF CHILDREN'S HEALTH CARE MINNEAPOLIS

(opposite)
Design Firm: Bozell

*Frankly,
we need support
in other areas.*

Corset, circa 1894.

**WESTERN
HERITAGE
MUSEUM**

Join the Western Heritage Museum and do more than remember. We're making history with exciting events like *Christmas at Union Station*, *Community* and *Omaha at Work*. For membership information, contact your company representative _____.

Design Firm: João Machado Design
Creative Director,
Designer: João Machado

Client: SMAS de Almada
(Municipal Water Services)
Poster celebrates National Water Day

A água no bom caminho

Design Firm: Nesnadny + Schwartz
Creative Director, Designer:
Gregory Oznowich
Photographer: Sanford Gross

Writer: Elizabeth Fowler
Printer: Watt Printing
Client: Cleveland Zoological
Society

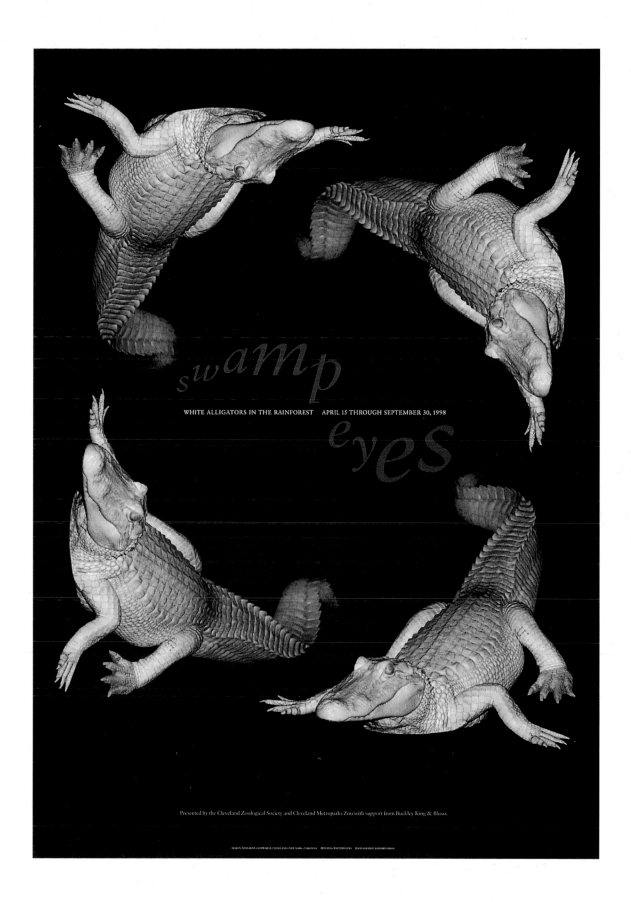

swamp eyes

WHITE ALLIGATORS IN THE RAINFOREST   APRIL 15 THROUGH SEPTEMBER 30, 1998

Presented by the Cleveland Zoological Society and Cleveland Metroparks Zoo with support from Buckley King & Bluso.

Design Firm: Imboden Melchior
Creative Director, Designer:
Imboden Melchior
Printer: Siebdruck Boeschag
Client: Art Museum of Lucerne

KUNSTMUSEUM LUZERN

KNOEBEL

Design Firm: Imboden Melchior
Creative Director, Designer:
Imboden Melchior
Printer: Siebdruck Boeschag
Client: Museum of History, Stans

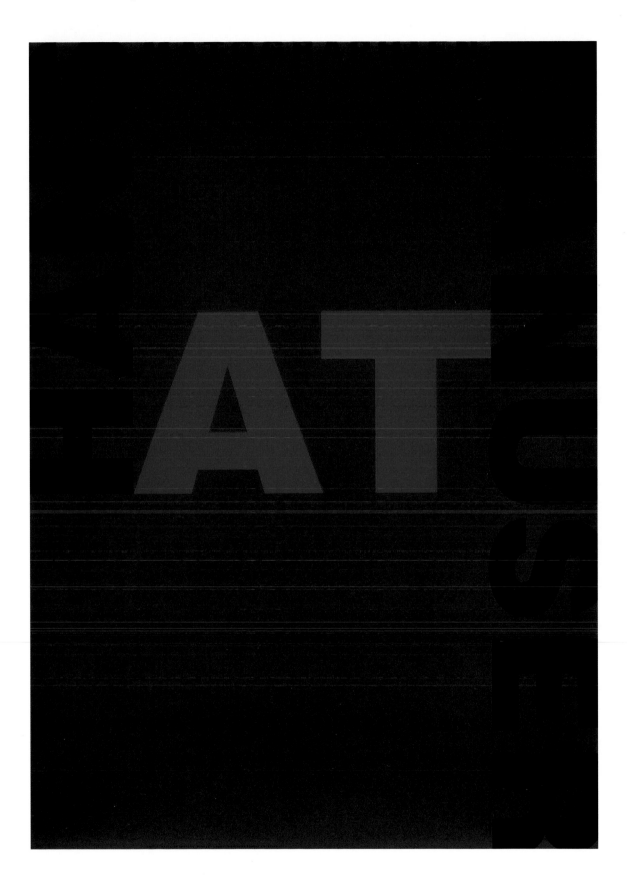

SAVE

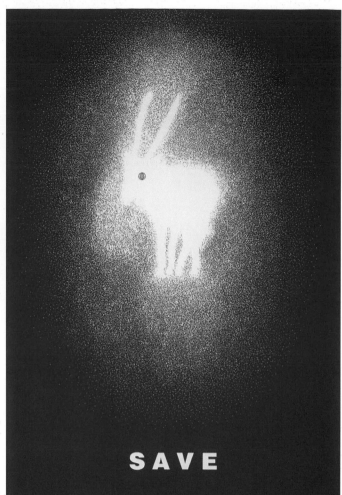

SAVE

SAVE

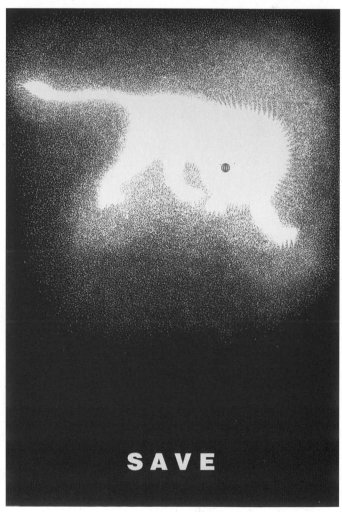

SAVE

(previous spread, this page)
Design Firm: Nippon Design
Center, Inc.
Creative Director, Designer:
Kazumasa Nagai
Self–exhibition

Design Firm: BEK
Creative Director, Writer:
Bülent Erkmen
Printer: Ofset Printhouse
Client: Berliner Ensemble
Exhibition for Brecht's 100th Birthday

This poster is designed to remind you of Bertolt Brecht's 100th birthday on February 10th. 1998

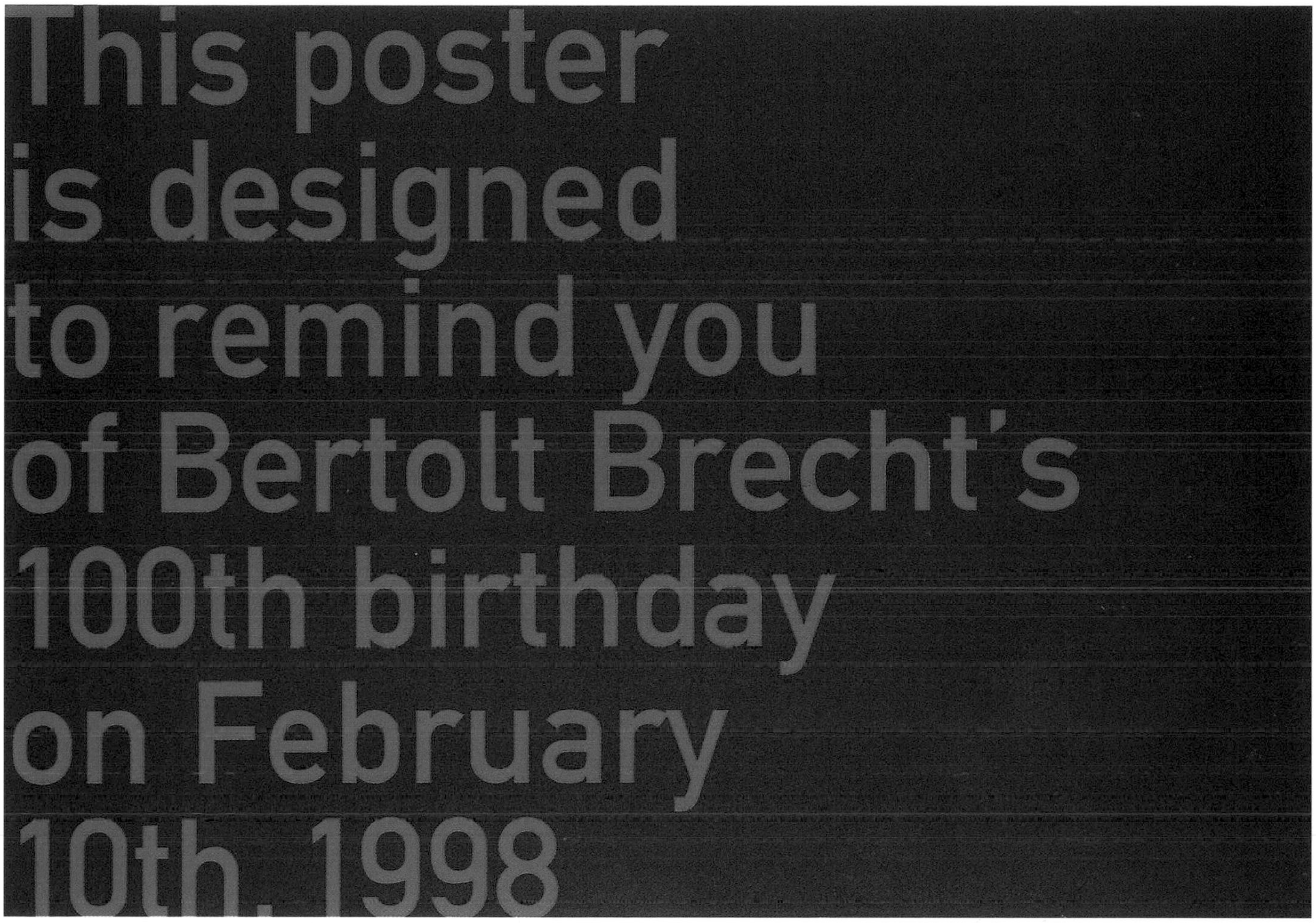

Creative Director: Kan Tai-Keung
Illustrator: C. K. Wong
Printer: Yu Luen Offset Printing
Client: Hong Kong Trade Council

Hong Kong Trade Development Council
SANTA MONICA PLACE

HONG
KONG
ART
SHOW
IN LA

A PROGRAMME OF "HELLO HONG KONG"

28 OCT - 20 NOV 1994 • SANTA MONICA PLACE

ORGANIZED BY HONG KONG TRADE DEVELOPMENT COUNCIL

SPONSORED BY SANTA MONICA PLACE • CITY OF SANTA MONICA

Design Consultants
Creative Director, Designer:
Kan Tai-Keung
Computer Illustrator:
Benson Kwun Tin Yau
Printer: G. L. Graphic Co. Ltd.

Homage to Paul Rand   Message from Kan Tai-keung   靳 埭 強   Hong Kong, China

(this spread)
Design Firm: Packaging Create Inc.
Art Director: Akio Okumura
Designer: Mitsuo Ueno
Client: Oji Paper Co. Ltd.
"Red and Black exhibition posters"

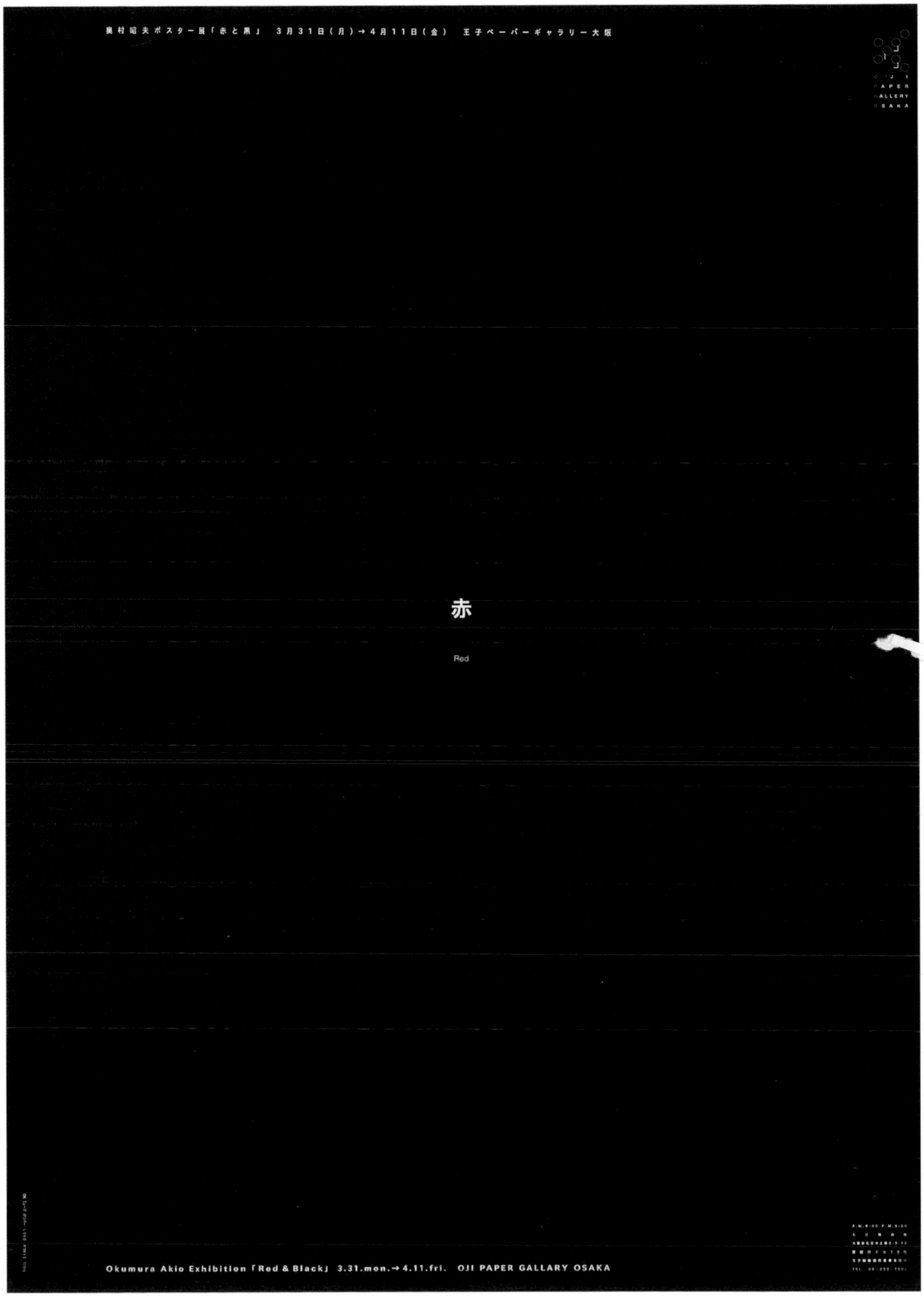

奥村昭夫ポスター展「赤と黒」 3月31日(月)→4月11日(金) 王子ペーパーギャラリー大阪
赤
Red
Okumura Akio Exhibition「Red & Black」 3.31.mon.→4.11.fri. OJI PAPER GALLARY OSAKA

Design Firm: Yokoo's Circus Co. Ltd.
Art Director, Designer: Tadanori Yokoo
Design Production: Studio Magic
Client: Takashimaya Dept.
Tadanori Yokoo "Counterattack of
Design Works" exhibition

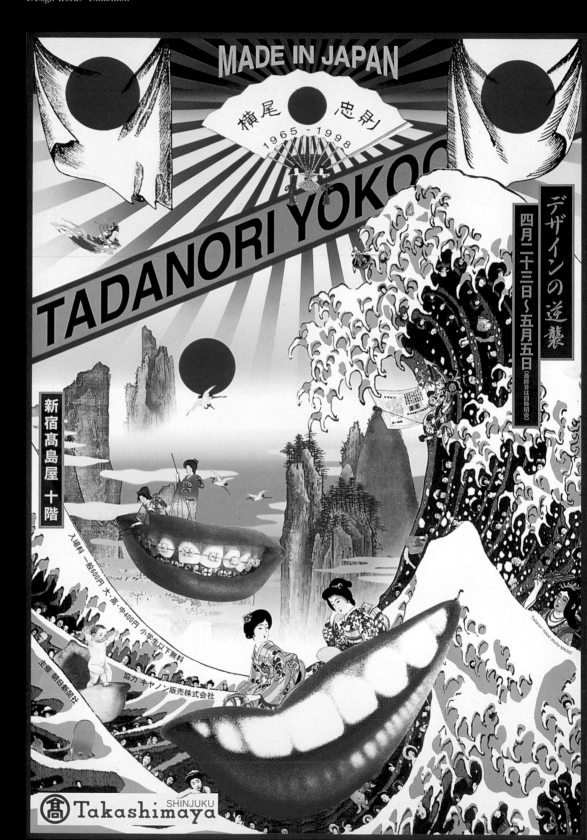

Design Firm: Shinnoske Inc.
Creative Director: Shinnoske Sugisaki
Art Directors: Shusuke Fukuzaki,
Shuichi Miyagishi
Designers: Jun Itadani, Chiaki Okuno

Photographer: Hiroyuki Yagyu
Printer: Koyo-Sha
Client: WcLock Gallery,
Digitalogue Gallery

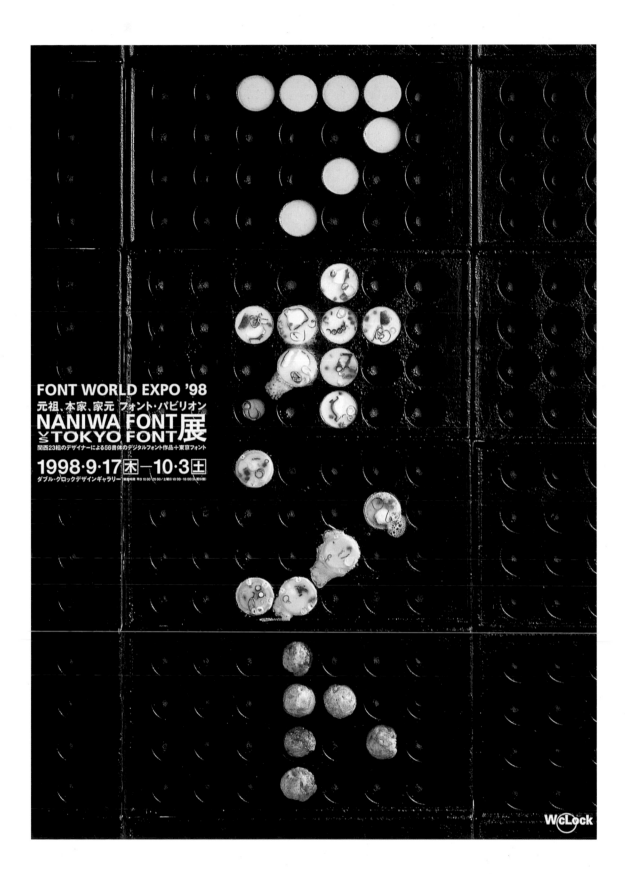

(this page)
Design Firm: Fons M. Hickmann
Art Director, Designer:
Fons M. Hickmann
Photographer: Nicola Schudy
Client: Guaredisch I
Exhibition for French-German
Artitsts' Collaboration

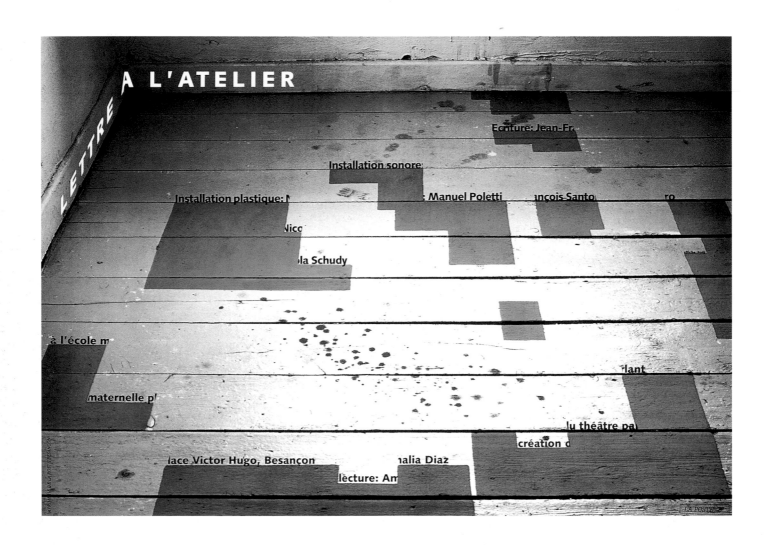

(opposite)
Design Firm: Kan & Lau
Design Consultants
Creative Director, Designer:
Kan Tai-Keung
Photographer: C. K. Wong
Computer Illustrator:
Benson Kwun Tin Yau
Printer: Hong Kong Prime
Printing Co. Ltd.
Client: Regional Council,
Hong Kong

asia-pacific posters exhibition
1997
03 nov - 01 dec 1000am-800pm daily*Exhibition Gallery,Sha Tin Town Hall,1 Yuen Wo Road,Sha Tin*Free Admission
Jointly presented by the Provisional Regional Council,Hong Kong and the Hong Kong Designers Association

Design Firm: Odermatt & Tissi
Designer: Rosmarie Tissi
Printer: Silkprint Spillmann, Zurich
Client: Swiss Poster Advertising Co.

Art Director, Designer: Luca Stoppini
Photographer: Peter Lindbergh
Client: Palazzo delle Esposizioni, Rome
Agent: Michele Filomeno
Exhibition of Lindbergh's photos

Art Director, Designer:
Yoshimaru Takahashi
Client: Osaka 21st Century Association
Bid for 2008 Olympics

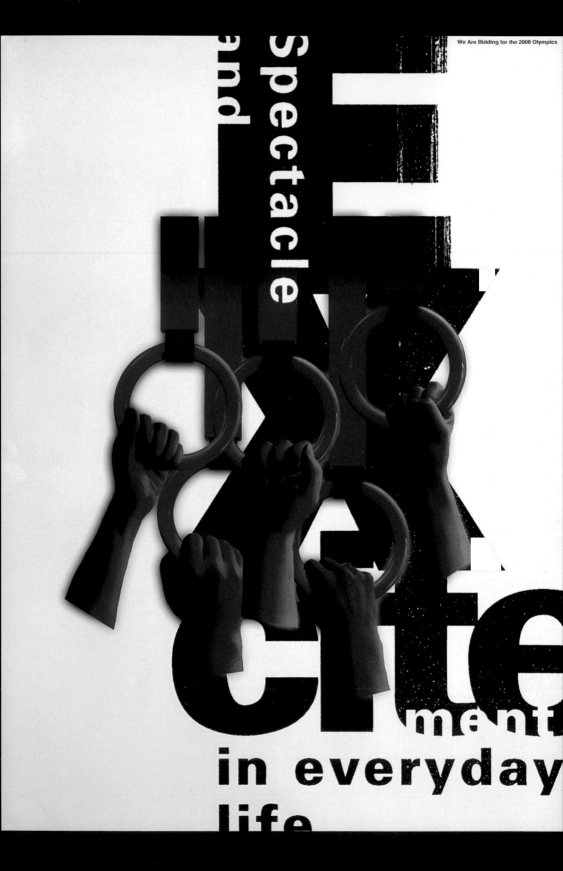

We Are Bidding for the 2008 Olympics

Spectacle and citement in everyday life

(opposite)
Design Firm: Luba Lukova Studio
Designer, Illustrator: Luba Lukova
Printer: Iznio, NY
Client: Contemporary
Illustrator's Gallery

(this spread)
Creative Director, Designer:
Uwe Loesch
Client, this page: Museum für
Kunsthandwerk Frankfurt am Main
Client, opposite: Ruhrlandmuseum Essen

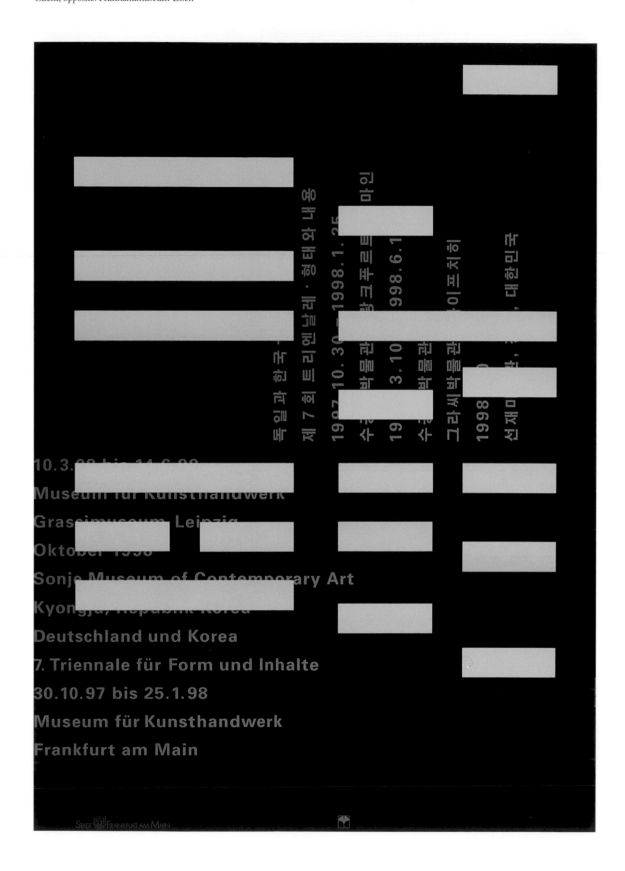

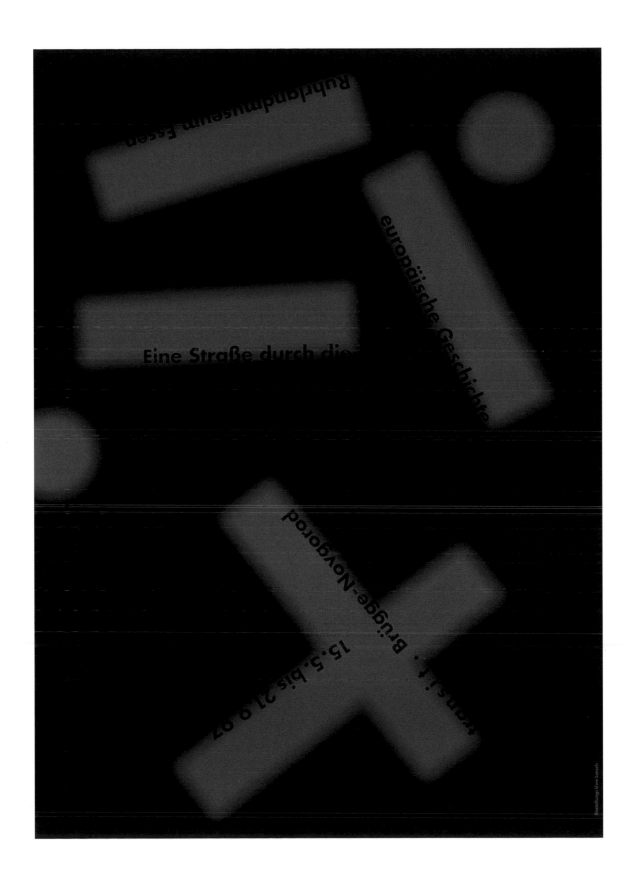

(opposite)
Design Firm: Skolos/Wedell
Creative Director, Designer:
Nancy Skolos
Printer: Daniels Printing
Client: Reinhold Brown Gallery

eXhibiToR sHoW 97

(this page)
Design Firm: Vanderbyl Design
Client: Exhibitor Magazine

(this page, top)
Design Firm: Savas Cekic
Tasarim Limited
Creative Director, Designer:
Savas Cekic
Client: Yurt & Dunya Art
Gallery

(this page, bottom)
Design Firm: Savas Cekic
Tasarim Limited
Creative Director, Designer:
Savas Cekic
Client: Mustafa Horasan

(opposite, top)
Design Firm: Savas Cekic
Tasarim Limited
Creative Director, Designer:
Savas Cekic
Client: Yurt & Dunya Art Gallery
Exhibition of Turkish painting
and sculpture

(opposite, bottom)
Design Firm: Savas Cekic
Tasarim Limited
Creative Director,
Art Director,
Designer: Savas Cekic
Client: Mine-Fatma Ünsal
Artist's exhibition

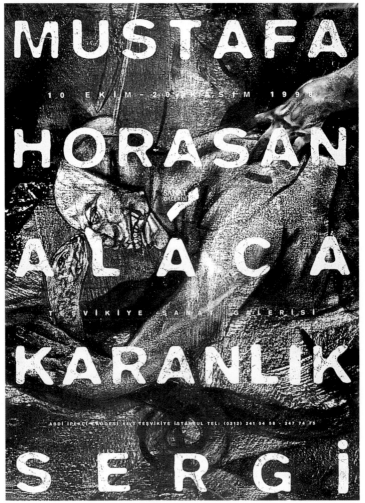

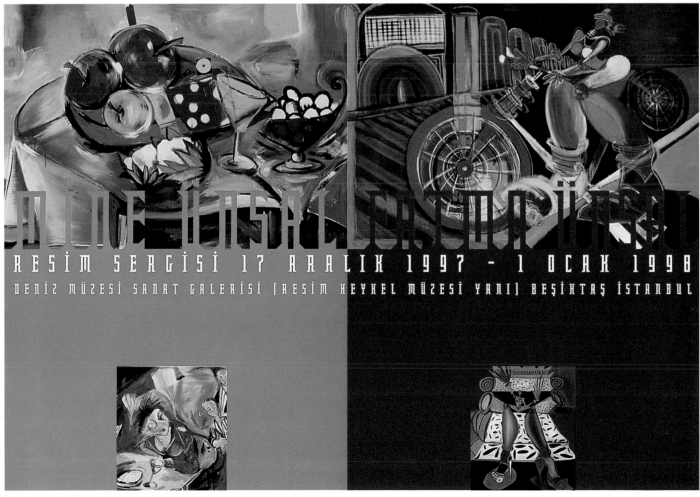

Design Firm: Zimmermann
Crowe Design
Creative Director, Designer:
Neal Zimmermann
Photographer: James Omara
Client: Levi Strauss & Co.

Design Firm: Zimmermann
Crowe Design
Creative Director: Neal Zimmermann
Designers: Neal Zimmermann,
Eric Heiman
Client: Levi Strauss & Co.

(this page)
Design Firm: Turner Duckworth
Design Consultants
Creative Directors: David Turner,
Bruce Duckworth
Designer: Jeff Fassnacht
Client: Levi Strauss & Co.

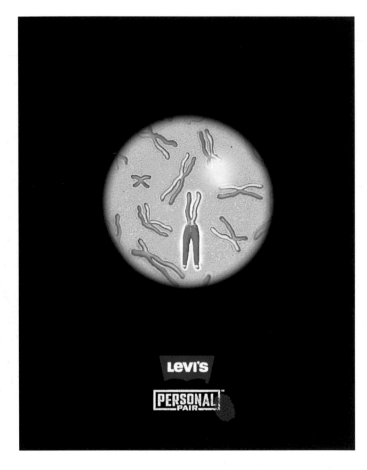

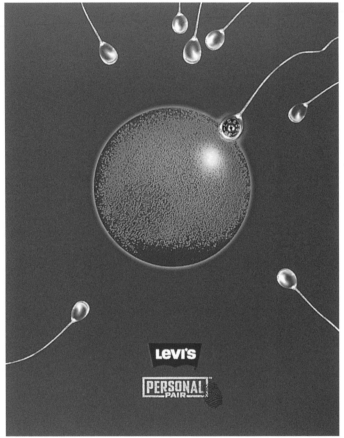

(opposite)
Design Firm: Corporate Profiles
Creative Director, Designer: Jacek Dyga
Photographer: Tomek Sikora
Writer: Hubert Stadnicki
Client: Levi Strauss Poland

Levi's 534
GORĄCA
para

RED
TAB
czer-
wona wszywka

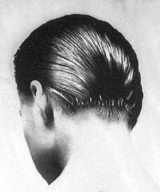

DOPASOWANE
SPODNIE
DLA DZIEWCZYNY

MA
1997 S
AGAП

MASUNAGA 1997
ART BY TAKO SAITO

(this spread)
Design Firm: Brey Graphics
Designer: Manfred Brey
Photographer: Markus Thommen
Series of three posters for Botty Basel

Design Firm: Shin Matsunaga
Design Inc.
Creative Director, Designer:
Shin Matsunaga
Client: Interntional Ceramics Festival
'98 Committee

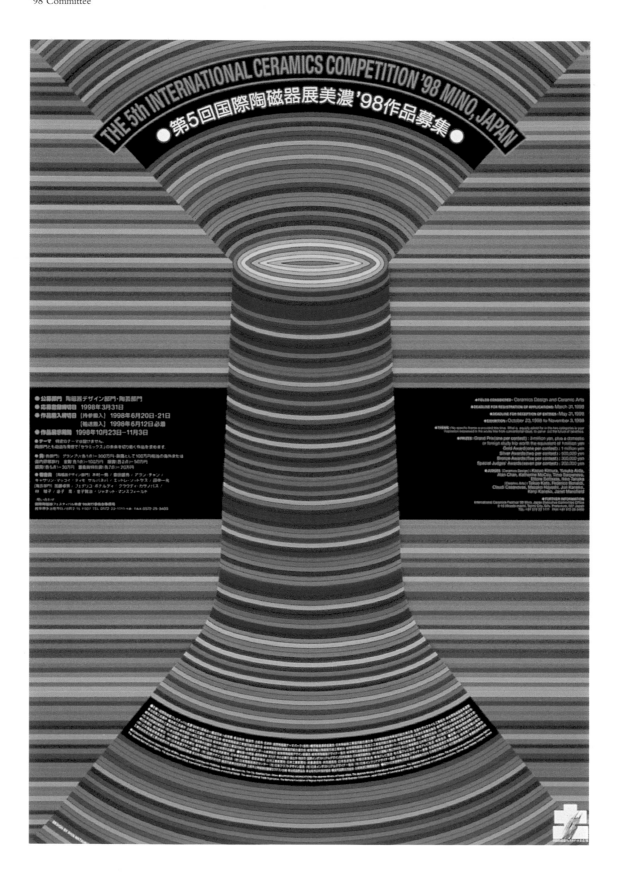

Design Firm: Kokokumaru Inc.
Art Director, Designer:
Yoshimaru Takahashi
Client: National Culture Festival
in Oita '98
Working Committee

BUDA

KONCERTEK: KONGRESSZUSI KÖZPONT · BM DUNAPALOTA · PESTI VIGADÓ · FRANCIA INTÉZET · ZENEAKADÉMIA

PESTI

FILM: HUNNIA · BROADWAY · URÁNIA · BEM · CORVIN · TOLDI · OLIMPIA · GRAFFITI

ŐSZI

KIÁLLÍTÁSOK: MŰCSARNOK · MAGYAR NEMZETI GALÉRIA · SZÉPMŰVÉSZETI MÚZEUM · BUDAPEST KIÁLLÍTÓTEREM

FESZ

SZÍNHÁZ: EGYETEMI SZÍNPAD · MERLIN · KOMÉDIUM · JÁTÉKSZÍN   FÜGGETLEN SZÍNPAD

TIVÁL

(opposite)
Art Director, Designer: Peter Vajda
Client: Autumn Festival, Budapest

(this page)
Design Firm: Colorful Stones
Creative Director, Designer:
Wempy Homeric
Photographer: Kervi Luo
Printer: Heidelberg Quickmaster DI 46-4
Client: The City of Savannah
Department of Cultural Affairs

POTATO FOOD
BAKED GOODS
JUMPING GYM
BUNGEE SLIDE
CRAFT PROJECTS
PONY RIDES
POTATO GAMES
FACE PAINTING
PETTING ZOO
HAUNTED HOUSE

ADULTS $5, CHILDREN FREE

10th ANNUAL · HAMPTON DAY SCHOOL

POTATO FESTIVAL

SATURDAY, OCT. 18, 11 TO 4 *

BUTTER LANE, BRIDGEHAMPTON

* RAIN DATE SUNDAY OCTOBER 19, 11 TO 4

(opposite)
Design Firm: Pentagram Design
Art Director, Designer: Woody Pirtle
Client: Hampton Day School

(this page)
Design Firm: Emery Vincent Design
Creative Director, Art Director:
Garry Emery
Client: Melbourne International
Festival of Art

Design Firm: Global Doghouse
Creative Directors:
Pamela Rodi, Steve Perani
Art Director:
Mary Evelyn McGough

Designers: Dela Erickson,
Ron Derhacopian
Writer: Micky Marx
Illustrator: Dean McCreary
Client: Sony Pictures

Design Firm: Global Doghouse
Creative Directors:
Pamela Rodi, Steve Perani
Art Director:
Mary Evelyn McGough

Designers: Dela Erickson,
Ron Derhacopian
Writer: Micky Marx
Illustrator: Dean McCreary
Client: Sony Pictures

Design Firm: Mires Design
Creative Director,
Art Director: José Serrano
Designers: Deborah Hom, José Serrano
Illustrator: Tracy Sabin
Client: Industry Pictures

THE REELS OF
INDUSTRY

Rolling into action!

INDUSTRY PICTURES

641 WEST LAKE STREET, SUITE 100, CHICAGO
ILLINOIS 60661 312-648-0505 FAX 312-648-4220

SUSAN KINAST, DIRECTOR

BRIAN CLARE, DIRECTOR

CLIFF GRANT, EXECUTIVE PRODUCER

CANDACE GELMAN, REPRESENTATIVE

Design Firm: Schraivogel Design
Designer: Ralph Schraivogel
Client: Zurich Film Podium

ELMA

GARCIA

FILMS

(opposite)
Design Firm: Michael Schwab Studio
Designer, Illustrator: Michael Schwab
Client: Elma Garcia Films

(this page)
Design Firm:
Carmichael Lynch Thorburn
Creative Director,
Photographer: Bill Phelps
Designer: Chad Hagen
Writer: Jonathan Sunshine
Client: Association of Children's
Healthcare

20th PORTLAND INTERNATIONAL
FILM FESTIVAL—13 FEB to 2 MAR

PRODUCED BY
NORTHWEST FILM CENTER
PORTLAND ART MUSEUM
©1997 USA

CREATIVE
DIRECTION. STEVE SANDOZ   DESIGN. SANDSTROM DESIGN, INC.   PHOTOGRAPHS. MARK HOOPER   PREP AND
                                                                                                    PRINTING. IRWIN-HODSON CO.

(opposite)
Design Firm: Sandstrom Design
Creative Director, Art Director:
Steve Sandstrom
Illustrator: Mark Hooper
Client: NW Film Center

(this page)
Creative Director, Designer: Uwe Loesch
Client: FilmKunstFestival Schwerin
Film Festival

TEQUILA

MEXICO

(opposite)
Design Firm: Garza Group
Communications
Designer: Agustin Garza

Photographer: Pico Gil
Printer: Scott Printing
Client: Mexican Ministry of Tourism

(this page)
Design Firm: Sandstrom Design
Creative Director, Art Director,
Designer: Steve Sandstrom

Illustrators: Maira Kalman,
Seymour Chwast, Greg Clark, Jeff Foster,
Jessie Hartland, John Hersey
Client: Einstein Bros. Restaurant

Figure 72a: TAZO FILTER-PACKED TEAS
(origin: Macedonia, 237 AD)

Three of several flavors created using the formulas discovered in the late 1960's during an archaeological exploration of Red Sea caves made possible by a lunar eclipse and the resultant abnormally low tides. Flavors include: Awake, Calm, Earl Grey, Passion, Spice, Refresh, Wild Sweet Orange and Zen.

TAZO är LIKA KALLT som SJÄLVA SVERIGE!

006

—REALLY, REALLY ICED TEA.

Figure 006: TAZO FROZEN TEA BARS
(Origin: Pyrenees Mountains, France, 600 AD)

A frozen confection originally produced by Basque mountain people who would pour Tazo concentrate into icy glacial holes to produce a more refreshing form of Tazo for the summer months.

Items 27 and 29 are Tazo Tea Bars representing some of the flavors which have been recreated for modern consumption: Wild Sweet Orange, Tazoberry, Passion Potion, Simply Red and Chai.

Item 29 is an ancient, partially eaten Tazo Tea Bar that was discovered by an expedition exploring the northern Pyrenees in 1984. The stick adjacent to this sample was found at the same time, but unfortunately the Tazo on it was consumed by one of the expedition members back at base camp. While he regretted the destruction of such an important find, he did say that it had been quite delicious.

ASIEN-WOCHEN

JAM JAM

JAM JAM

BEI McDONALD'S

(this page)
Design Firm: Heye & Partners
Creative Director: Alex Bartel

(this page)
Design Firm: Mudra
Communications Ltd.
Designer: B. Ramnathkar
Client: McDonald's

(opposite)
Design Firm: Pontificia
Universidad Católica
Creative Director: Ximena Ulibarri
Designer: Ximena Ulibarri
Printer: Ograma S. A.
Client: Embotelladora Andina S. A.
Bottlers of Coca-Cola products

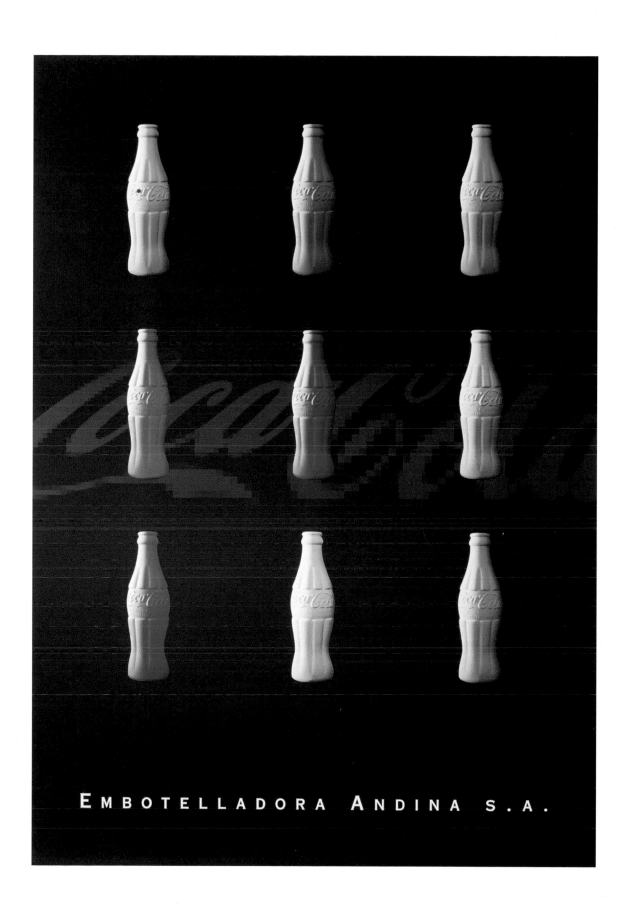

EMBOTELLADORA ANDINA S.A.

BREAD IS MADE
FOR LAUGHTER,
AND WINE
GLADDENS LIFE.

ECCLESIASTES
10:19

(opposite)
Design Firm: Michael Schwab Studio
Art Director: Deb Miller
Designer, Illustrator: Michael Schwab
Printer: B&R Screen Graphics

Agency: VNO Design
Client: American Cancer Society
One of three posters showing role of
wine in religion

(this page)
Design Firm: Saint Hieronymus
Press, Inc.
Creative Director, Designer, Illustrator:
David Lance Goines
Client: Chez Panisse

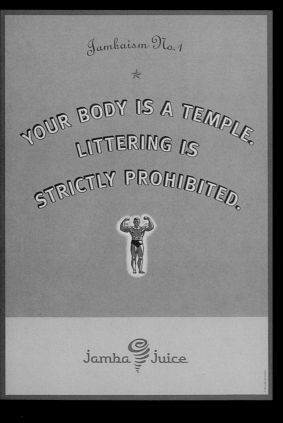

(top right)
Design Firm: Butler, Shine & Stern
Creative Directors: John Butler,
Mike Shine

Art Director: Hilary Wolfe
Writer: Dean Wei
Illustrator: Leigh Wells
Client: Jamba Juice

(opposite, bottom)
Design Firm: Butler Shine & Stern
Creative Directors: John Butler,
Mike Shine

Art Director: Hilary Wolfe
Writer: Ryan Ebner
Illustrator: Leigh Wells
Client: Jamba Juice

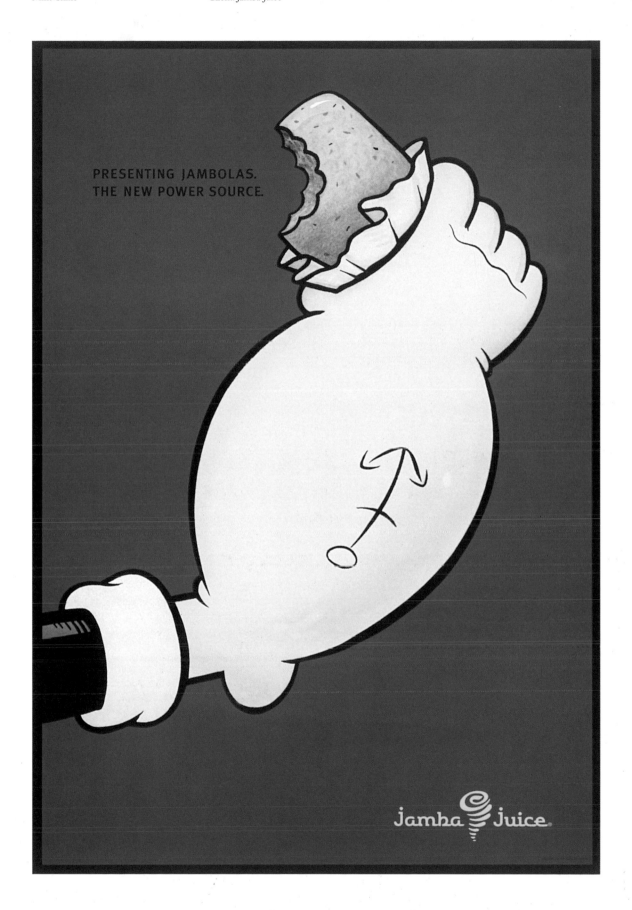

(this page)
Design Firm: Butler, Shine & Stern
Creative Directors: John Butler,
Mike Shine

Art Director: Hilary Wolfe
Writer: Ryan Ebner
Illustrator: Harry Bliss
Client: Jamba Juice

OPEN

ANGEL LAND FUKUI

福井県児童科学館

EL MUSEO
MEXICANO

celebrating twenty years of art and culture

(opposite)
Design Firm: Morla Design
Creative Director, Designer:
Jennifer Morla
Printer, Client: Bacchus Press

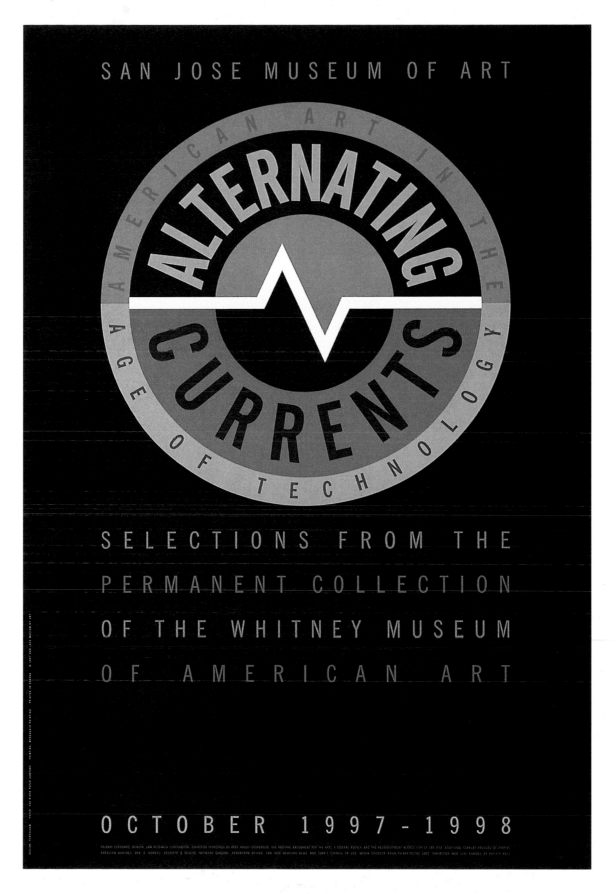

(this page)
Design Firm: Pentagram Design Inc.   Designer: David Asari
Creative Director, Art Director: Printer: MacDonald Printing
Kit Hinrichs   Client: San Jose Museum of Art

Design Firm/Agency: Cole & Weber
Creative Director: Ron Klein
Art Director, Designer,
Photographer: Steve Rudasics

Writer: Kevin Jones
Illustrator: Fred Johnson
Printer: Boeing Print Shop
Client: The Museum of Flight

Art Director, Designer:
Harumi Kirima
Photographer: Shunmei Miyake
Client: I.F. Company
Poster for musician

(this spread)
Design Firm: Niklaus Troxler Design
Creative Director, Designer, Illustrator:
Niklaus Troxler
Printer: Boesch Siebdruck
Client: Jazz In Willisau
Jazz Concert

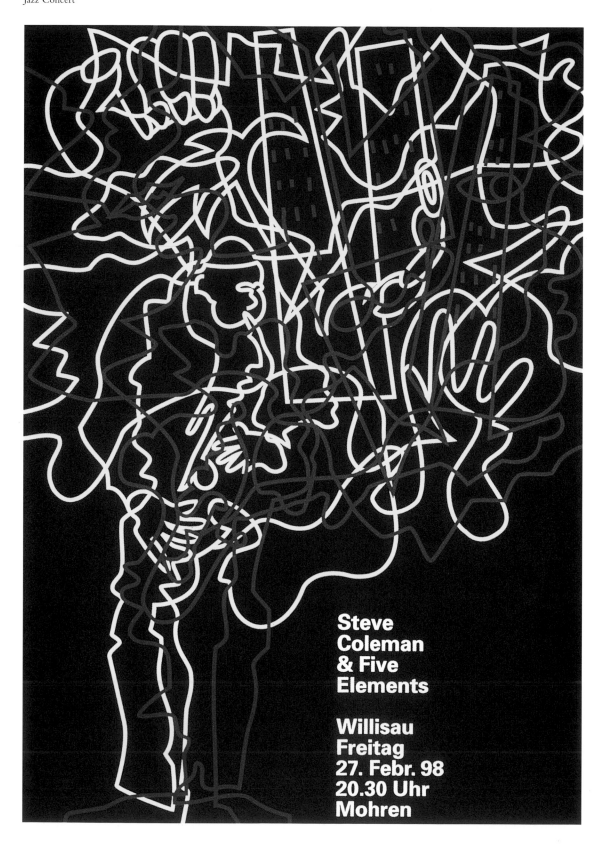

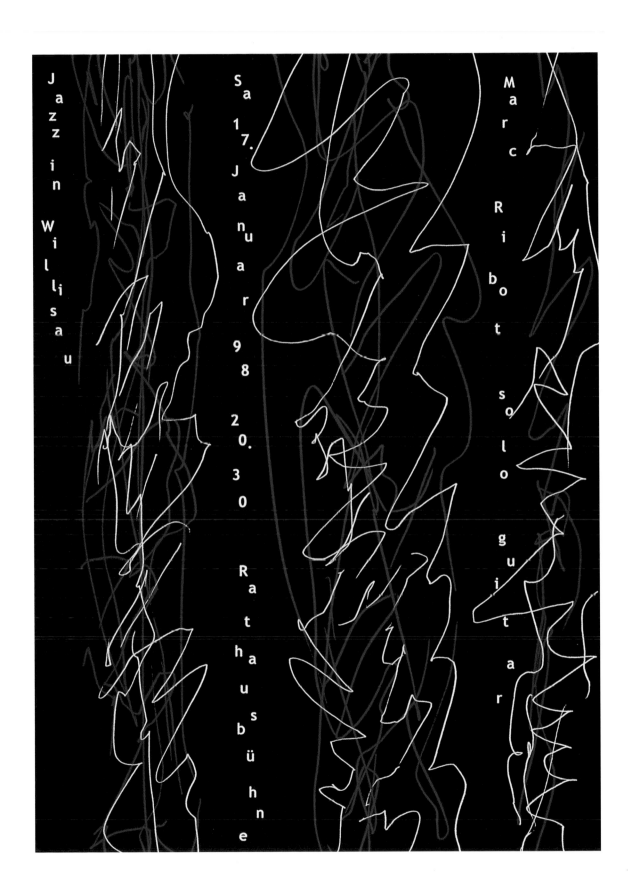

Dallas Symphony Orchestra 1997 European Tour Andrew Litton, Music Director

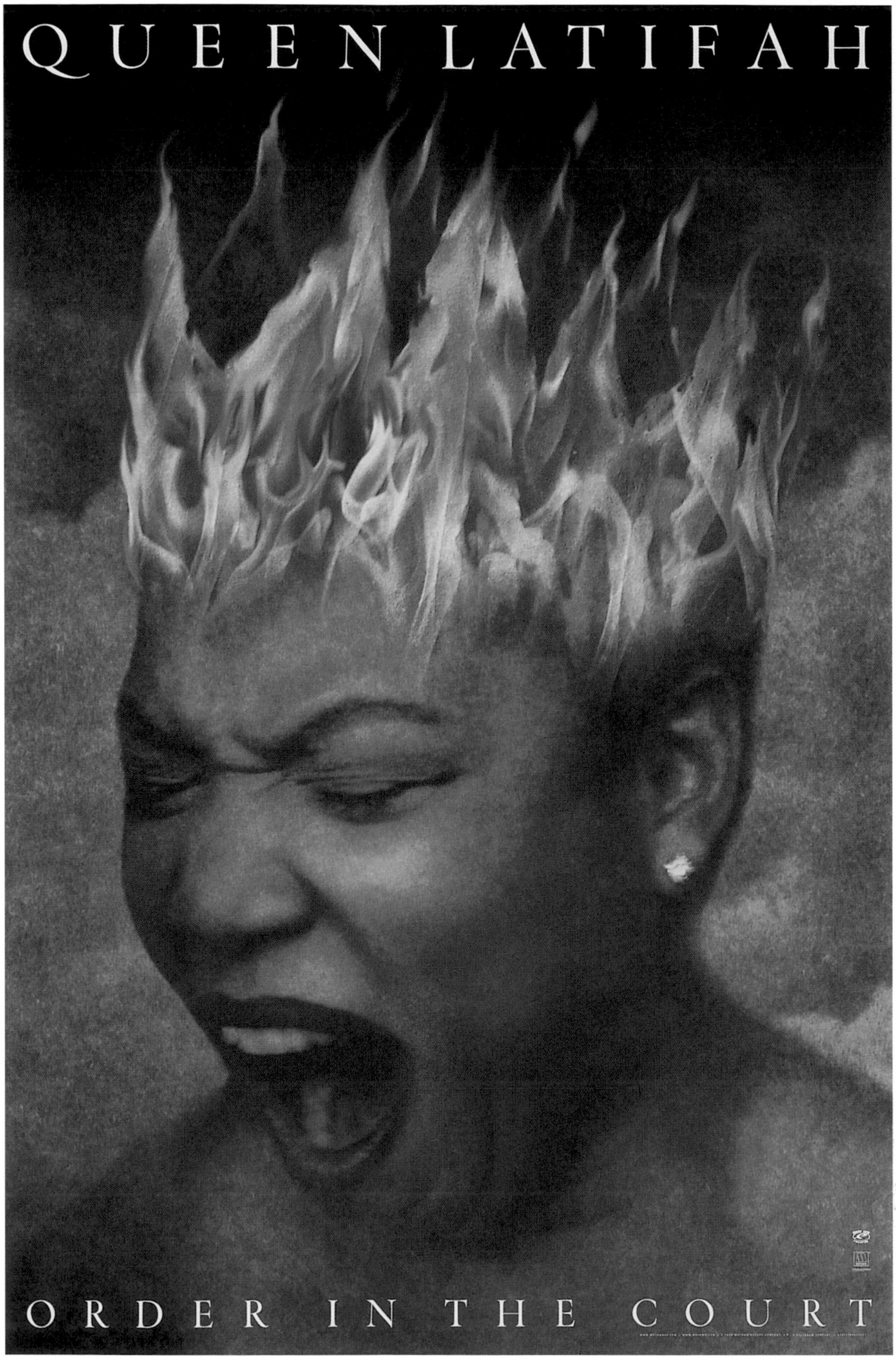
QUEEN LATIFAH
ORDER IN THE COURT

(opposite)
Design Firm: Motown Records
(in-house)
Art Directors: David Harley,
David Irvin
Designer: David Harley
Photographer: Matt Mahurin
Client: Queen Latifah
Album release

(this page)
Design Firm: Motown Records
(in-house)
Art Directors: David Irvin,
David Harley
Designer: Jin Kim
Illustrator: McDavid Henderson
Client: Diana Ross
Artist of the month campaign

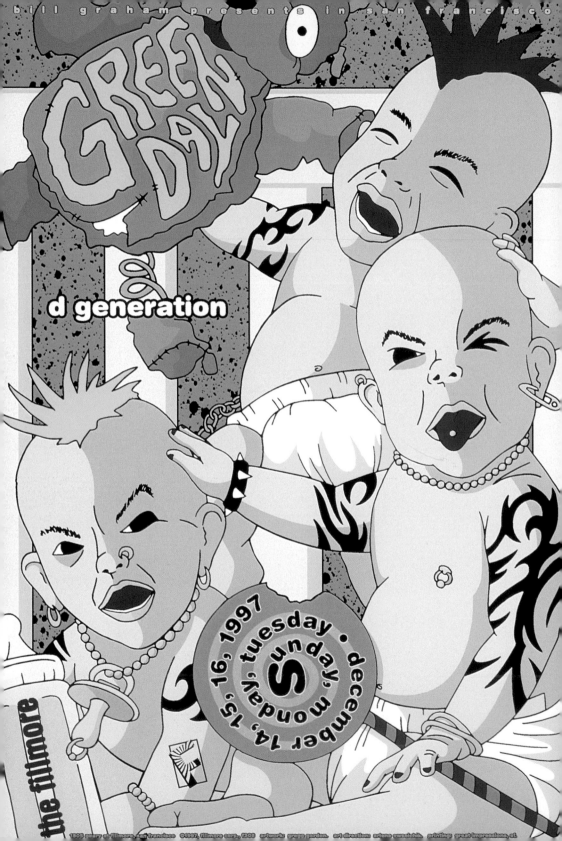

(this page)
Design Firm: Muller & Co.
Creative Director, Designer:
John Muller
Art Director: Mark Voss
Photographer: Mike Regnier
Illustrator: John Muller
Client: KC Blues & Jazz Festvial

THE FOUNDATION FOR ARCHITECTURE
1996 BEAUX ARTS BALL

TOP BRASS
NAVY BLUES
& BOOGIE WOOGIE

at the Naval Business Center

SATURDAY
OCTOBER 19, 1996
9:30PM TO 2:00AM

THE PHILADELPHIA NAVAL
BUSINESS CENTER
FORMERLY THE PHILADELPHIA
NAVY BASE
AT THE SOUTH END
OF BROAD STREET

COME JITTERBUG IN
RED, WHITE AND BLUE.

DRESS IN COSTUME OR BLACK TIE.
WEAR A MASK OR A HAT.
JOIN IN THE COSTUME PARADE
HOSTED BY WMMR'S PIERRE ROBERT.

FOR TICKET INFORMATION,
CALL TICKETMASTER,
1-215-336-2000

HOSTED BY THE PHILADELPHIA INDUSTRIAL DEVELOPMENT CORPORATION WITH SPECIAL THANKS TO THE US NAVY

(opposite)
Design Firm:
McAdams, Richman & Ong
Creative Director, Designer:
Randall Jones

Photographer: Paul Crane
Client: The Foundation
for Architecture

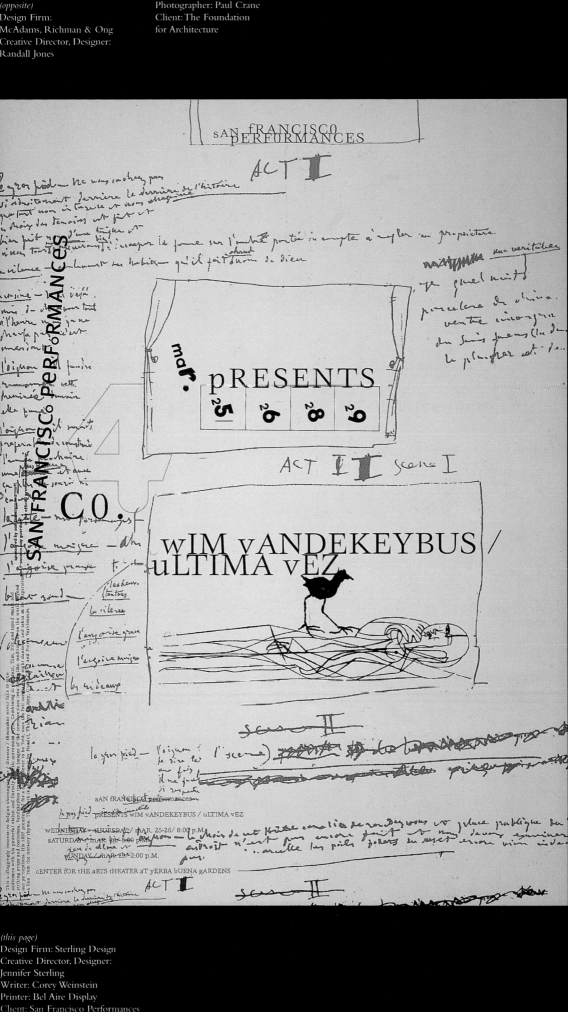

(this page)
Design Firm: Sterling Design
Creative Director, Designer:
Jennifer Sterling
Writer: Corey Weinstein
Printer: Bel Aire Display
Client: San Francisco Performances

Design Firm: Primo Angeli Inc.
Creative Director, Designer:
Primo Angeli
Illustrator: Chotima Buranabunpot
Client: San Francisco Boys Chorus

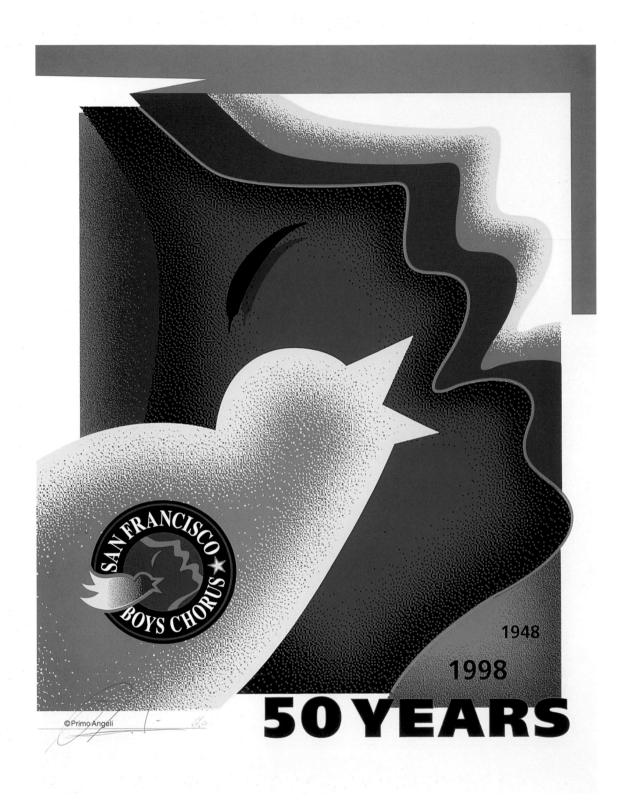

Design Firm: After Hours Creative
Printer: Sierra Screen Print
Client: Maricopa Community
College District

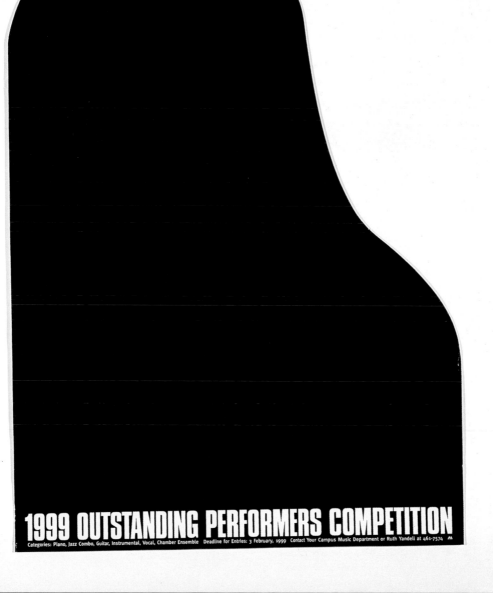

1999 OUTSTANDING PERFORMERS COMPETITION

Categories: Piano, Jazz Combo, Guitar, Instrumental, Vocal, Chamber Ensemble   Deadline for Entries: 3 February, 1999   Contact Your Campus Music Department or Ruth Yandell at 461-7574

Design Firm: Sagmeister Inc.
Creative Director, Designer:
Stefan Sagmeister
Photographer:
Timothy Greenfield Sanders

Text: Lou Reed
Printer: WEA
Client: Warner Bros. Music

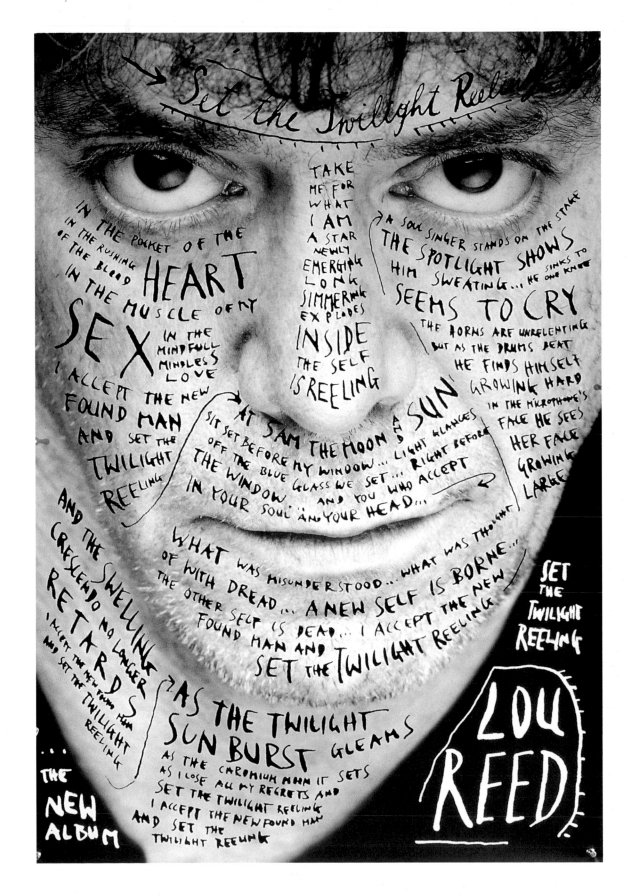

Design Firm:
Charles S. Anderson Design Co.
Art Director: Charles S. Anderson
Designer: Todd Piper-Hauswirth
Photographer:
Eric Emmings, CSA Plastock
Client: Wisconsin Paper Company

Design Firm: Milton Glaser Inc
Designer: Milton Glaser
Client: Via Marketing & Design

Premium

HEMP PAPER

Another Tree Free Paper From

Green Field Paper Co.

100% RECYCLED · 70 LB/180 GSM · 40 PAGES · ACID FREE · MADE IN THE USA

ANSEL ADAMS

MOUNT McKINLEY RANGE · DENALI NATIONAL PARK · ALASKA

PEACE
A HUMAN
RIGHT
HAGUE APPEAL
FOR PEACE
MAY 11-15, 1999
THE HAGUE
OFFICE 777 UN PLAZA
NEW YORK, NY 10017
TEL: 212 687 2623
hap99@igc.apc.org
www.haguepeace.org
or, c/o IALANA, Anna
Paulownastraat 103,
2518 BC The Hague,
THE NETHERLANDS
tel +31 70 363 4484
ialana@antenna.nl

NO

GO

THE HAGUE APPEAL FOR PEACE IS SUPPORTED IN PART BY GRANTS FROM THE MINISTRY OF FOREIGN AFFAIRS, HOLLAND, BARBARA M. WALKER, THE JOHN D. AND CATHERINE T. MACARTHUR FOUNDATION, LIFEBRIDGE FOUNDATION, PAUL AND DAISY SOROS FOUNDATION, SAMUEL RUBIN FOUNDATION, STEWART MOTT CHARITABLE TRUST

Creative Director, Designer, Client:
Uwe Loesch

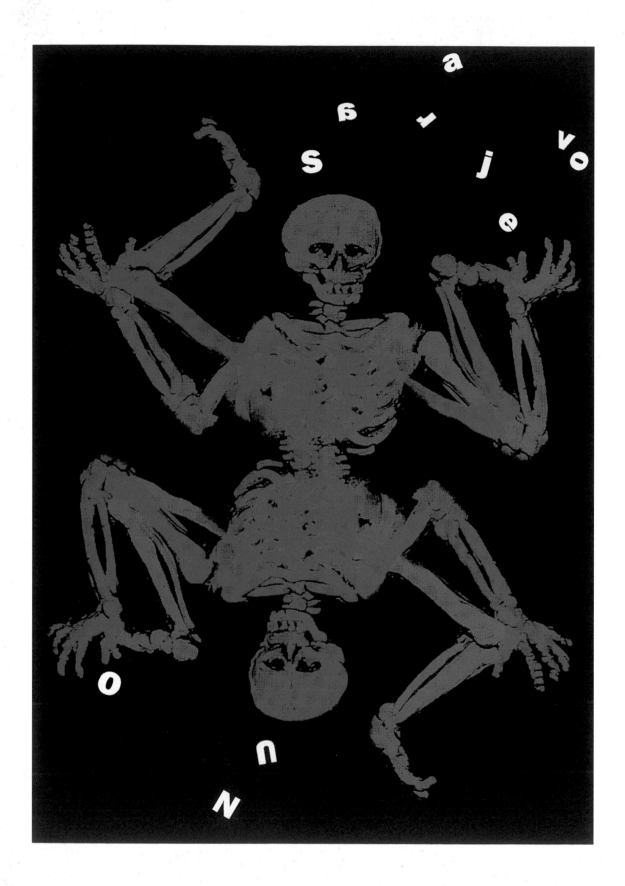

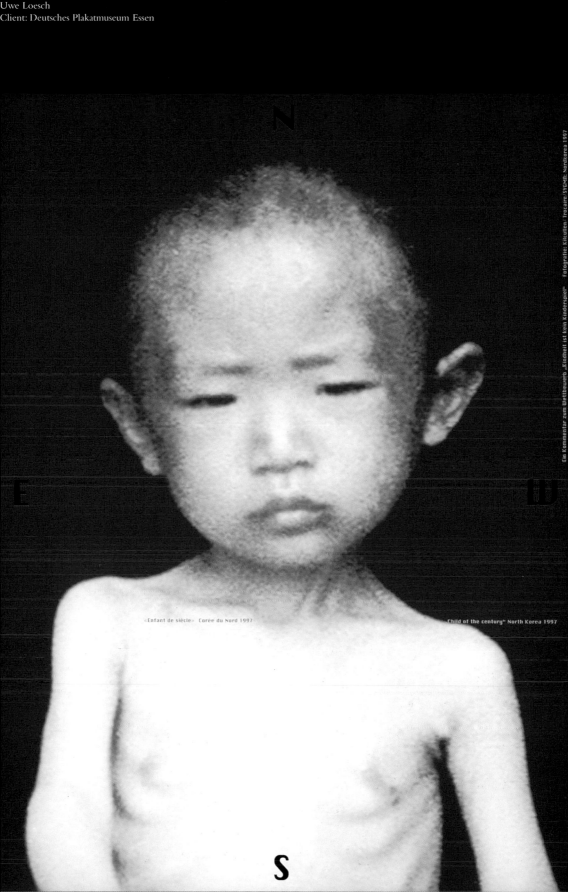

N

E

W

«Enfant de siècle» Corée du Nord 1997

Child of the century" North Korea 1997

Ein Kommentar zum Wettbewerb „Kindheit ist kein Kinderspiel" Fotografie: Kibuilen Trocaire (SVGdH; Nordkorea 1997

S

PROFANITY

Creative Director, Art Director,
Designer: Savas Cekic
Client: Emegin Partisi/Political
Party of Labor

(this page)
Design Firm/Agency: Initio
Creative Director: Scott Sample
Art Director, Designer: Derek Sussner
Photographer: Elle Kingsbury
Writer: Jeff Mueller
Printer, Client: Heartland Graphics

(opposite)
Design Firm:
Charles S. Anderson Design Co.
Art Director: Charles S. Anderson
Designers: Charles S. Anderson,
Erik Johnson
Photographer: Steve Belkowitz
Printer: Litho Inc.

Photo by *STEVE BELKOWITZ*

Waterless printing by Litho Inc., St. Paul, MN 612.644.3000. Paper supplied by The French Paper Co., Niles, MI 616.683.1100. Design by Charles S. Anderson Design Co., Minneapolis, MN 612.339.5181, Copy by Lisa Pomrick. Photography by Steve Belkowitz Photography, Philadelphia, PA 215.629.1802.

(this spread)
Design Firm: Hoffman York
Creative Director, Writer: Tom Jordan
Art Director, Designer: Ken Butts
Photographer: Dave Jordano
Client: Mautz Paint

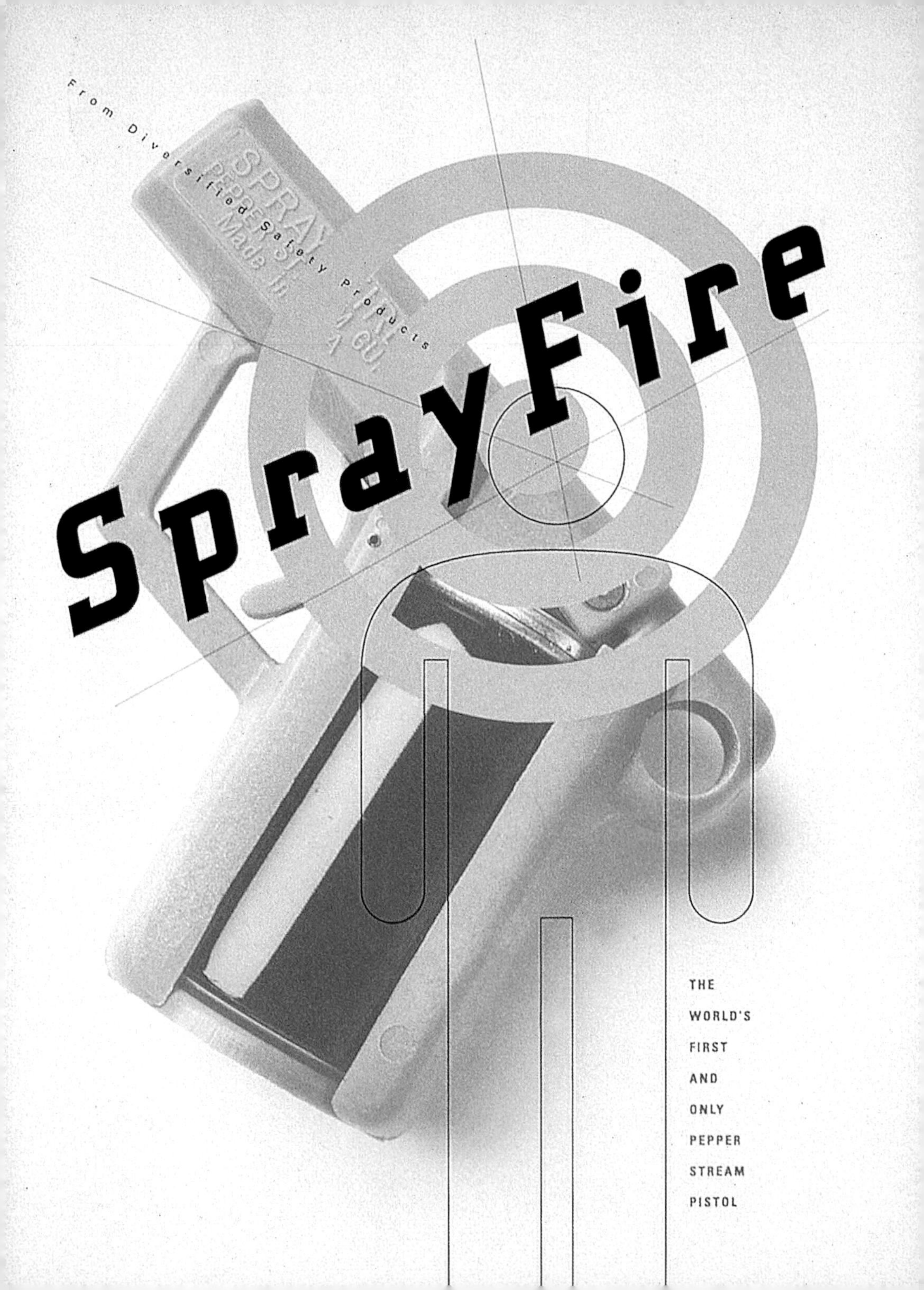
From Diversified Safety Products
SprayFire
THE WORLD'S FIRST AND ONLY PEPPER STREAM PISTOL

THIS IS THE CAP MELISSA WEAVER WAS GIVEN THE DAY SHE GRADUATED FROM LIFEGUARD TRAINING. TWO WEEKS LATER, SHE PULLED CRAIG WATKINS FROM THE BOTTOM OF HER LOCAL SWIMMING POOL AND WATCHED HER HANDS WORK INSTINCTIVELY TO BREATHE HIS COLD BODY TO CONSCIOUSNESS. THE WAITING FAMILY CALLED HER A HERO. BUT MELISSA WOULDN'T HAVE KNOWN WHAT TO DO HAD HER CREDO BELONGED TO SOMEONE ELSE. WHAT CAN YOU OFFER THE AMERICAN RED CROSS?

ALL HUMAN BEINGS ARE BORN FREE AND EQUAL

Article I Universal Declaration of Human Rights, 1948

(opposite)
Design Firm: Titanium
Creative Director: Dann De Witt
Art Director: Maryalice Eckart
Photographer: Jana León
Printer: Acme Printing
Client: Reebok International

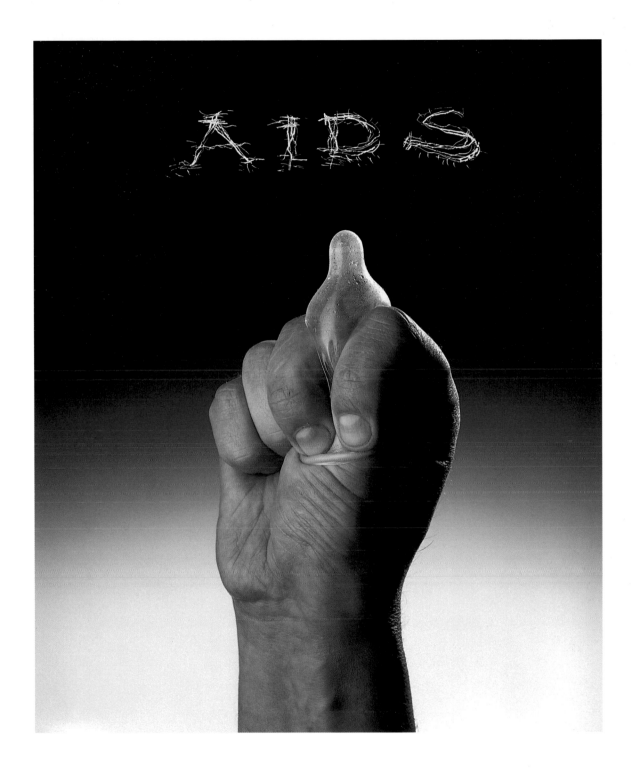

(this page)
Designer: Czeslaw Zuber
Photographer: D. Fradin

PEACE

(opposite)
Design Firm, Client:
Squires & Company
Creative Director: Paul Black

Art Director, Designer:
Brandon Murphy
Photographer: Doug Davis
Illustrator: Brian Taylor

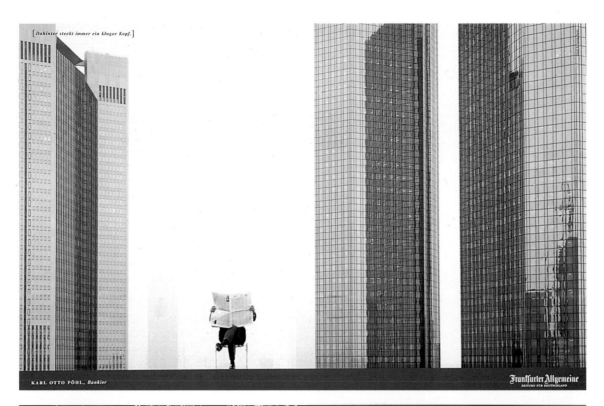

(this page)
Design Firm: Scholz & Friends
Creative Director, Art Director:
Petra Reichenbach
Photographer: Alfred Seiland
Writer: Sebastian Turner
Client: F.A.Z. Newspaper

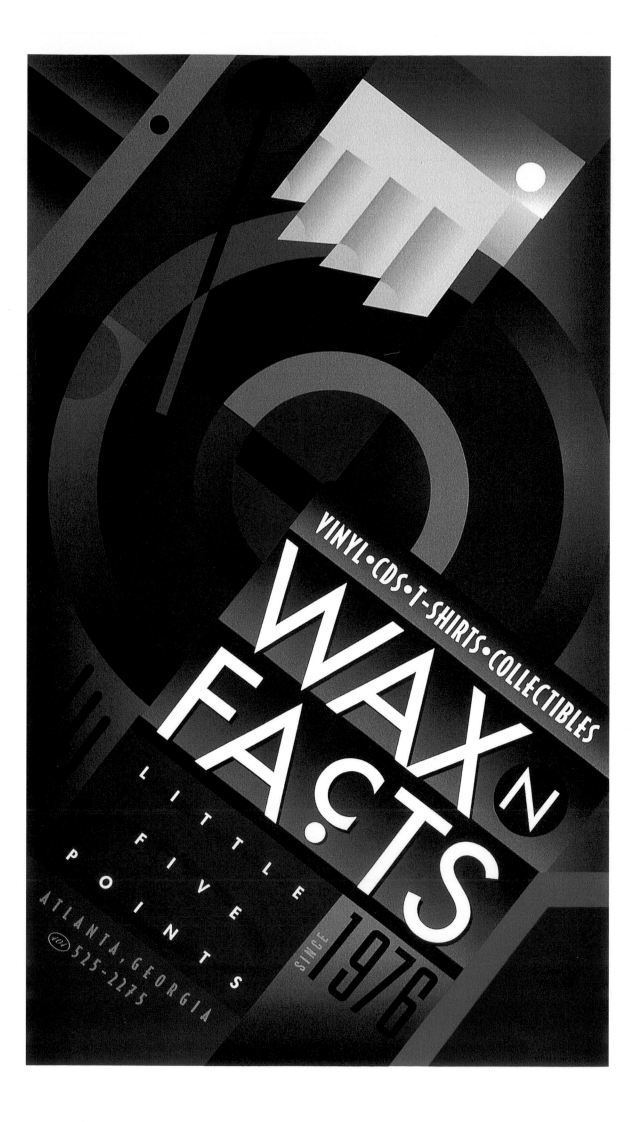

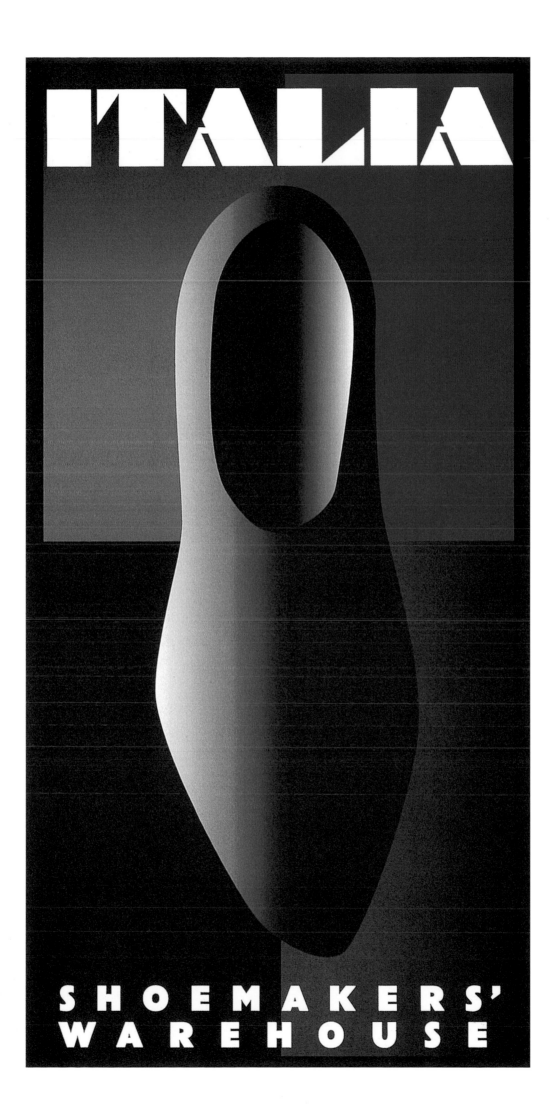

(previous spread, left page)
Design Firm: Banks Albers Design
Creative Director, Designer,
Illustrator: Scott Banks
Printer: TR Digital Productions

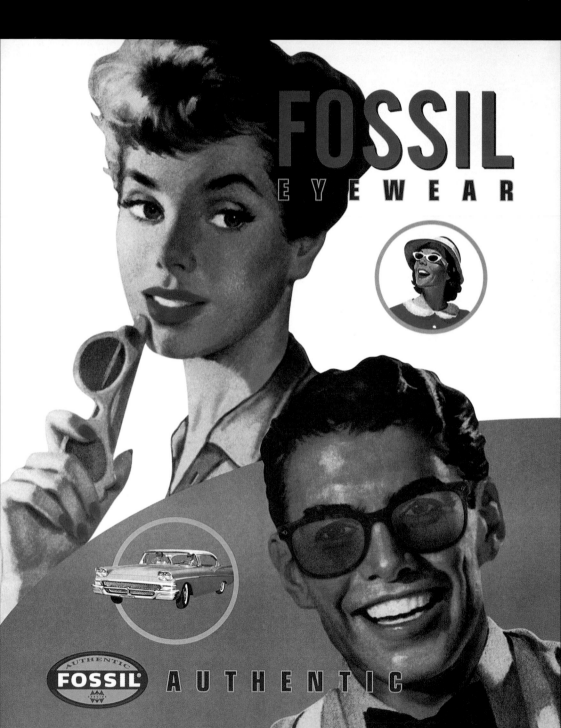

(opposite)
Design Firm, Client: Fossil
Creative Director: Tim Hale
Art Directors: Steven Zhang,
Clay Reed, Casey McGarr
Designer: David Eden

(this page)
Design Firm, Client: Fossil
Creative Director: Tim Hale
Art Directors: Steven Zhang,
Casey McGarr
Designer: David Eden

(this page)
Design Firm: Kenzo Izutani
Office Corporation
Art Director: Kenzo Izutani

Designers: Kenzo Izutani, Aki Hirai
Photographer: Yasuyuki Amazutsumi
Printer: Nimura Printing Inc.
Client: AT&T Jens Corp.

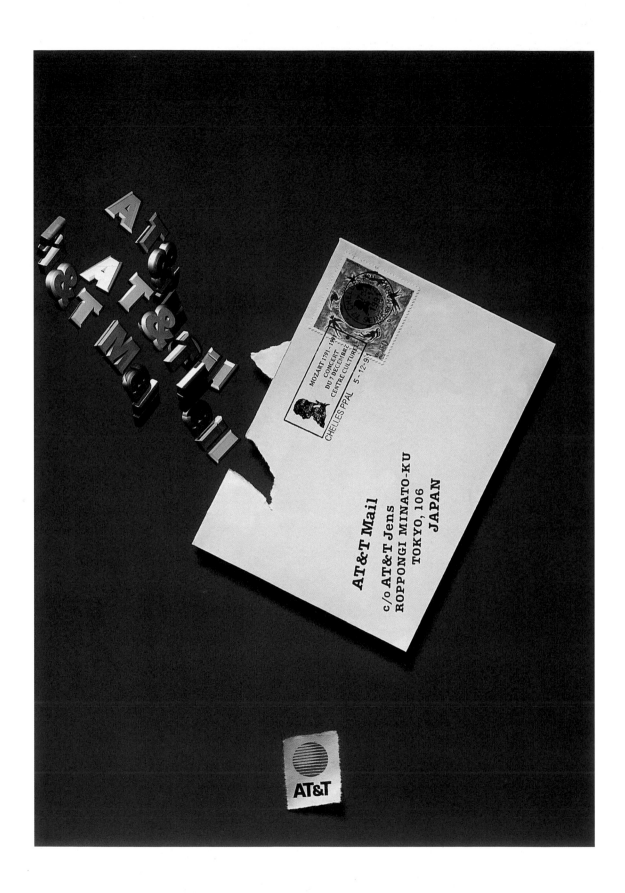

(opposite)
Design Firm: Michael Schwab Studio
Creative Director: Andy Dreyfus
Art Directors: Andy Dreyfus,

Michael Schwab
Designer, Photographer:
Michael Schwab
Client: American Presidents Line

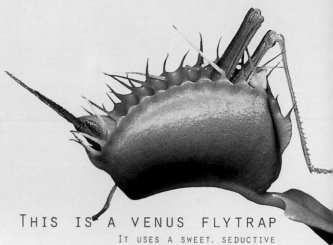

THIS IS A VENUS FLYTRAP

IT USES A SWEET, SEDUCTIVE
SCENT TO ATTRACT INSECTS
WE USE THE TELEPHONE
ONCE THE PREY IS TRAPPED
THERE IS NO ESCAPE
DITTO

DEBTORS ARE AN ELUSIVE GROUP.
TOUGH TO FIND. EVEN TOUGHER TO GET A HOLD OF.
THAT'S WHY WE'VE DEVELOPED A FULLY AUTOMATED
CALLER LOCATION SYSTEM TO HELP YOU LOCATE THEM.

BY INSTANTLY TRACING DEBTORS' CALLS TO A UNIQUE
800 NUMBER AND EXTENSION, OUR SYSTEM TRAPS THE NUMBER
THEY'RE CALLING FROM AND, IN MANY CASES, EVEN TELLS
YOU THE ADDRESS. YOU CAN HAVE THE INFORMATION FAXED TO YOU
TWICE DAILY, INSTANTANEOUSLY, OR YOU CAN BE CONNECTED DIRECTLY
WITH THE DEBTORS TO SPEAK WITH THEM. IT DEFEATS CALLER ID
BLOCKING AND DOES NOT REQUIRE YOU TO PURCHASE ANY EQUIPMENT.
OUR SYSTEM IS THE MOST COST EFFECTIVE SKIP-TRACING TOOL
AVAILABLE. IT'S FULLY AUTOMATED, OPERATES 24 HOURS A DAY,
AND OF COURSE, DOES NOT REQUIRE A GREEN THUMB.

TO RECEIVE A FREE BROCHURE OR DEMONSTRATION,
CALL US AT 1-800-360-5601 OR 1-714-479-0889.
ASSET AND OTHER SEARCHES ARE ALSO AVAILABLE.

U.S. TRACERS
INCORPORATED

(opposite)
Design Firm: Xeno Group Inc.
Creative Director,
Designer: Victor Wang
Client: U.S. Tracers Inc.

(this page)
Design Firm: BBDO/Vancouver
Creative Director, Art Director:
Rick Wakefield
Photographer: Chris Davis
Client: Ask Guy Tucker
Headhunter

KENTUCKY DERBY
FESTIVAL 1998

Design Firm: Sandstrom Design
Creative Director: Steve Sandstrom
Art Director: George Vogt
Illustrator: Michael Schwab
Printer: Premier Press
Client: Nike

Design Firm:
Studio Gianni Bortolotti & C.
Creative Director, Art Director,
Designer: Gianni Bortolotti
Client: CONI, Roma

Design Firm:
Studio Gianni Bortolotti & C.
Creative Director, Art Director,
Designer: Gianni Bortolotti
Client: CONI, Roma

SECTION	ROW	SEAT	ADMIT ONE	ALL SEATS RESERVED	No. 152
T-V TEE-VEE ROOM	F FRONT	IT'S YOUR HOUSE. SIT WHEREVER YOU DARN WELL PLEASE.		BUT YOU'LL ONLY NEED THE EDGE.	☞ ENTER REAR DOOR

SEE THE

ATHLETIC MARVELS! ENIGMAS of the EXTREME!

X GAMES

EXTRAORDINARY **BALANCE!**
SPLIT-SECOND **TIMING!**
MULTIPLE **BODY PIERCINGS!**

EXPERIENCE **CONSTANT** LOW-GRADE AMBIENT **PANIC** IN THE COMFORT OF YOUR OWN HOME!

7 DAYS OF GLORIOUS, **FIERCE** — AND — **CARNIVOROUS** COMPETITION

AN **ESPN** & **ESPN2** PRODUCTION

THE THRILLER SUPREME!
NO SPITTING.
DON'T MISS THIS ONE ☞

JUNE 24-30

★ RHODE ISLAND USA ★
NO EXTRA CHARGE
ETC, ETC, ETC.

SHEER UNADULTERATED ATHLETIC LUNACY SERVED UP FRESH & PIPIN' HOT

SKY SURFING
SURF'S UP. WAY, WAY, WAY UP!

IT'S SPIDER-RIFIC! SPORT CLIMBING

BICYCLE STUNT
STARK RAVIN' MAD!

BUNGY JUMPING
A FEARFUL FROLIC WITH FATE!

STREET LUGE
THE OFFICIAL PACE CAR OF **INSANITY**

SKATEBOARDING
A SPANDEX-FREE EVENT.

IN-LINE DOWNHILL
CLINICAL PSYCHOLOGISTS CAN ONLY DREAM ABOUT PEOPLE LIKE THIS!

AGGRESSIVE IN-LINE
SKATERS KNOWN NOT FOR THEIR TRIPLE LUTZS.

WAKEBOARDING AND BAREFOOT JUMPING
MOSES PARTED THE SEA WITH GOD'S HELP...THESE GUYS ARE ALL ON THEIR OWN.

EXTREME ADVENTURE RACE BLISTERS!!
250 MISERABLE MILES AND MORE BLISTERS THAN THE PAINT ON A SUN-BAKED MEXICAN CANTINA.

(opposite)
Design Firm: Sandstrom Design
Creative Director: Rob Palmer
Designer: Steve Sandstrom

Photographer: Jonathan Rosen
Writer: Jeff Bitsack
Client: ESPN

(this page)
Design Firm: Sandstrom Design
Creative Director: Steve Sandstrom
Art Director: Hal Curtis
Designers: Steve Sandstrom,

Michele Melandri
Writer: Jerry Cronin
Illustrator: Jeff Foster
Client: ESPN

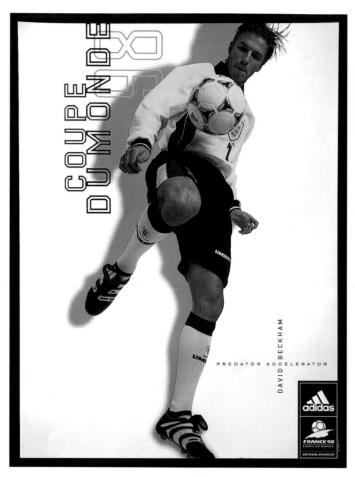

COUPE DU MONDE

PREDATOR ACCELERATOR

DAVID BECKHAM

adidas

FRANCE 98
OFFICIAL SPONSOR

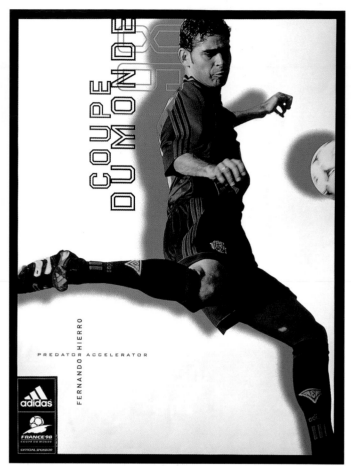

COUPE DU MONDE

PREDATOR ACCELERATOR

FERNANDO HIERRO

adidas

FRANCE 98
OFFICIAL SPONSOR

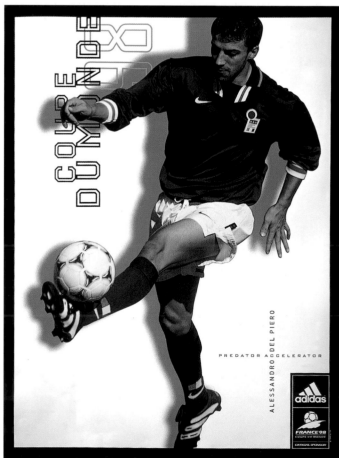

COUPE DU MONDE

PREDATOR ACCELERATOR

ALESSANDRO DEL PIERO

adidas

FRANCE 98
OFFICIAL SPONSOR

COUPE DU MONDE

PREDATOR ACCELERATOR

ZINEDINE ZIDANE

adidas

FRANCE 98

(this spread)
Design Firm: Sandstrom Design
Creative Director:
Steve Sandstrom
Art Director: Sally Morrow
Designer: Starlee Matz
Photographers: Walter Iooss,
C.B. Harding
Client: Adidas International

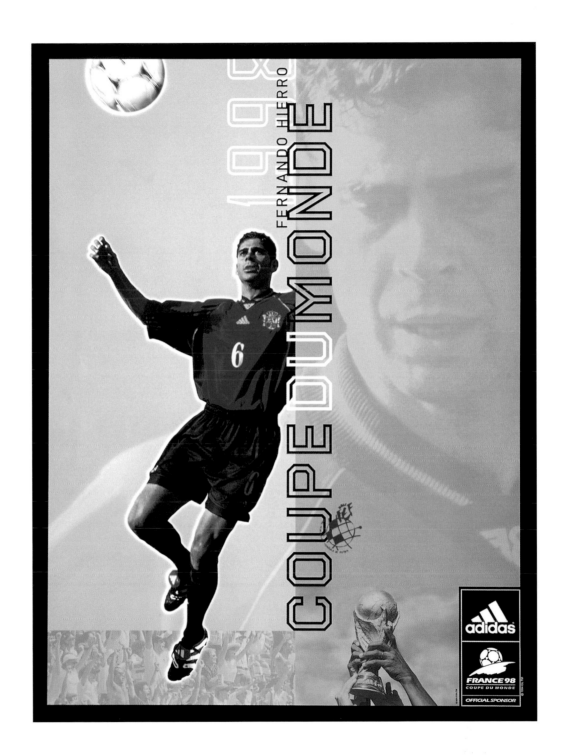

U T A G A T A R I
歌語り
［一休恋慕］
企画・原案＝小椋佳　音楽＝小椋佳・福井峻　音楽監督＝福井峻　演出＝福井泰司
演者＝伊藤多喜雄　東家浦太郎　岩崎晴龍　内山みゆき　松永栄子　刀根麻里子　小椋佳
平成10年7月20(月祝)　開場5：30PM　開演6：00PM　料金(税込)　S席5,500円　A席4,500円
足利市民会館
制作:トライアングル　協賛:セキスイハイム　協力:足利市民文化友の会　制作協力:足利おんきょう　主催:足利市教育委員会、(財)足利市体育・文化振興会　お問い合わせ:足利市民会館 電話0284-41-2121

(opposite)
Design Firm: Kokokumaru Inc.
Art Director, Designer:
Yoshimaru Takahashi

Art Director: José A. Serrano
Photographer: Tracy Sabin
Client: Irvine Barclay Theatre

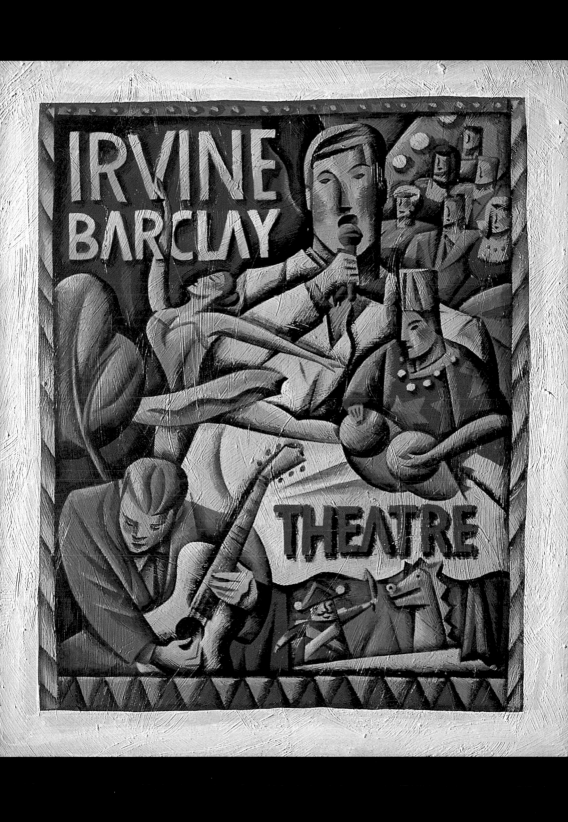

(this page)
Design Firm: Mires Design
Creative Director,
Art Director: José A. Serrano
Photographer: Tracy Sabin
Client: Irvine Barclay Theatre

BALLAD OF YACHIYO

BY PHILIP KAN GOTANDA

DIRECTED BY SHARO

THE

(opposite)
Design Firm: Pentagram Design
Art Director: Paula Scher
Designer: Anke Stohlman
Client: Public Theater

(this page)
Design Firm: Pentagram Design
Art Director: Paula Scher
Client: Public Theater

Design Firm: Holbeck
Kommunikationsdesign
Art Director, Illustrator, Designer:
Karina Holbeck
Client: Comedia Colonia, Cologne

Design Firm: Kari Piippo Oy
Creative Director, Designer,
Illustrator: Kari Piippo
Client: Jyväskylän Kaupunginteatteri
Children's play, "Beauty and the Beast"

KARI PIIPPO

KANSANSATU/SIRKKU PELTOLA Ohjaus Petri Lairikko

KAUNOTAR JA HIRVIÖ
JYVÄSKYLÄN KAUPUNGINTEATTERI

OYOUS
-Jack Tinker- London Daily Mail
ELEG NT!
John Lahr- The New Yorker
GENIUS!!
-Michael Sommers- The Star Ledger
ELECTRIC!
-Ben Brantley, The New York Times
-Joel Siegle, WABC TV
MAGIC!!
-Laura Shapiro, Newsweek
GLORIUS!
BRING IN 'DA NOISE
BRING IN 'DA FUNK
BREAKTHROUGH!
-Linda Winer- Newsweek
WONDERFUL!!
-Clive Barnes, NY Post
*WINNER- 4 1996 TONY AWARDS
EXPLOSIVE!
-Howard Kissel, Daily News
SIZZLING!
-Michael Kuchwara, Associated Press
THE PUBLIC THEATER ON BROADWAY
CALL TELE-CHARGE IN NY NJ/CT 212-239-6200
OUTSIDE NY METRO AREA 800-432-7250
THE AMBASSADOR THEATRE
219 WEST 49TH ST

(opposite)
Design Firm: Pentagram Design
Art Director: Paula Scher
Designer: Keith Daigle
Client: Public Theater

HOW I LEARNED TO DRIVE 1998 PULITZER PRIZE WINNER
WRITTEN BY PAULA VOGEL
DIRECTED BY MARK RUCKER

JULY 17TH - AUGUST 16TH
CALL 269-1900 OR 292-ARTS
LIFE'S LESSONS ARE RARELY BLACK & WHITE.

INTIMAN THEATRE
WARNER SHOOK-ARTISTIC DIRECTOR

(this page)
Design Firm: Cyclone
Designers, Photographers:
Traci Daberko, Dennis Clouse
Client: Intiman Theatre

(this page)
Design Firm: Mike Salisbury
Communications
Creative Director, Photographer:
Mike Salisbury
Art Directors: Mary McGough,
Mike Salisbury
Designer: Mary McGough
Client: Rage Magazine

(opposite)
Designer: Gary A. Williams, II,
Art Center College of Design
Text: Billy Corgan
Letterpress Exploration/
Personal Project

so may you come with your own knives

you'll never take me alive

with all the force of what is true

and the NIGHTmare rides on, and the NIGHTmare rides on, with a december black psalm, and the nightmare rides on

I've faced the fathoms in your deep

withstood the suitors quiet siege

pulled down the heavens just to please you   appease you the wind blows and I know

I can't go on digging roses from your grave

to linger on, beyond the beyond

to hold the flower I can't keep   where the willows weep and whirl

-pools sleep

you'll find me

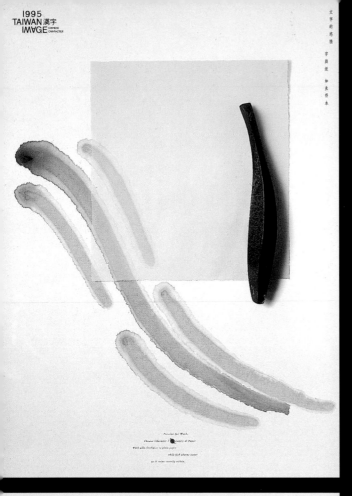

Passion for Words
Chinese Character (Nature) & Paper
Work adds liveliness to plain paper
while lush storms water
as it swims merrily within.

Passion for Words
Chinese Character (Winds) & Inkstone
The writhing movement of ink on inkstone
creates a feel of
lush, delightful wind.

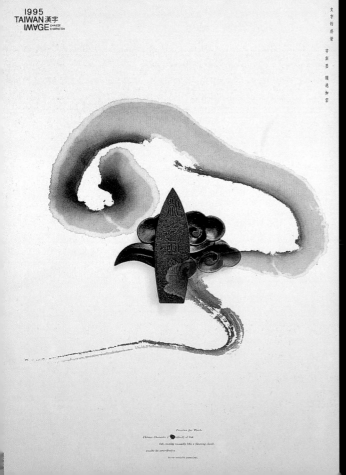

Passion for Words
Chinese Character (Handy) of Ink
Ink, moving nimbly like a fleeting cloud,
exalts the contribution
in an artistic creation.

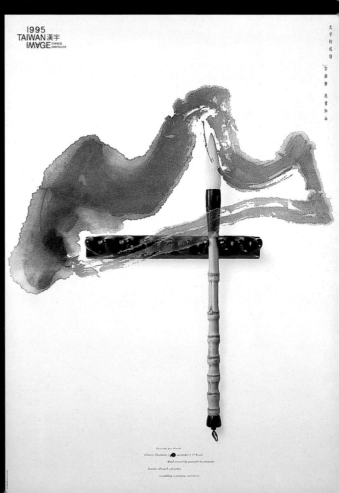

Passion for Words
Chinese Character (mountain) of Brush
Work smooth by powerful brushworks
beams strength and grace,
resembling a precious mountain.

Creative Director,
Designer: Kan Tai-Keung
Printer: Yu Luen Offset Printing
Client: Taiwan Image Poster

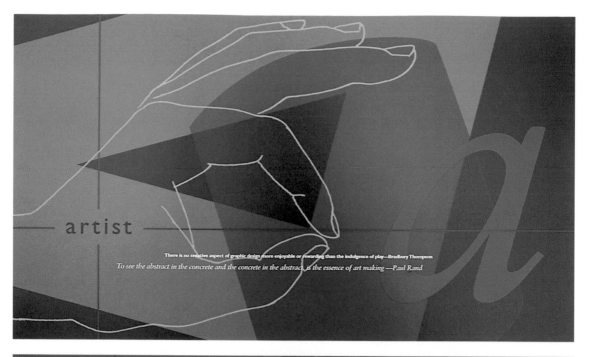

artist

There is no creative aspect of graphic design more enjoyable or rewarding than the indulgence of play—Bradbury Thompson

To see the abstract in the concrete and the concrete in the abstract, is the essence of art making—Paul Rand

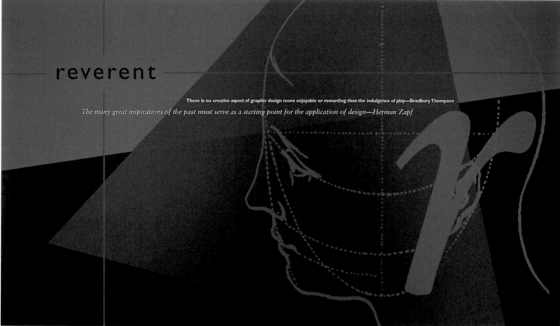

reverent

There is no creative aspect of graphic design more enjoyable or rewarding than the indulgence of play—Bradbury Thompson

The many great inspirations of the past must serve as a starting point for the application of design—Herman Zapf

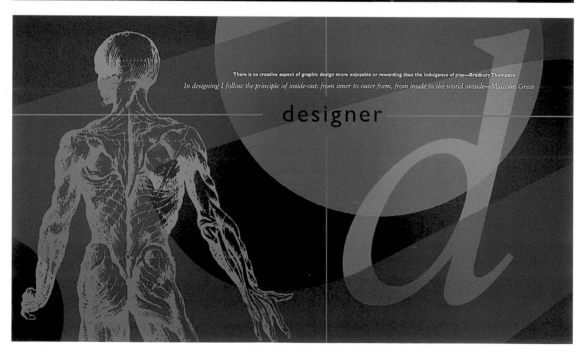

There is no creative aspect of graphic design more enjoyable or rewarding than the indulgence of play—Bradbury Thompson

In designing I follow the principle of inside-out: from inner to outer form, from inside to the world outside—Malcolm Grear

designer

(opposite)
Designer: Heather A. Snyder,
Rhode Island School of Design
Homage to Bradbury Thompson

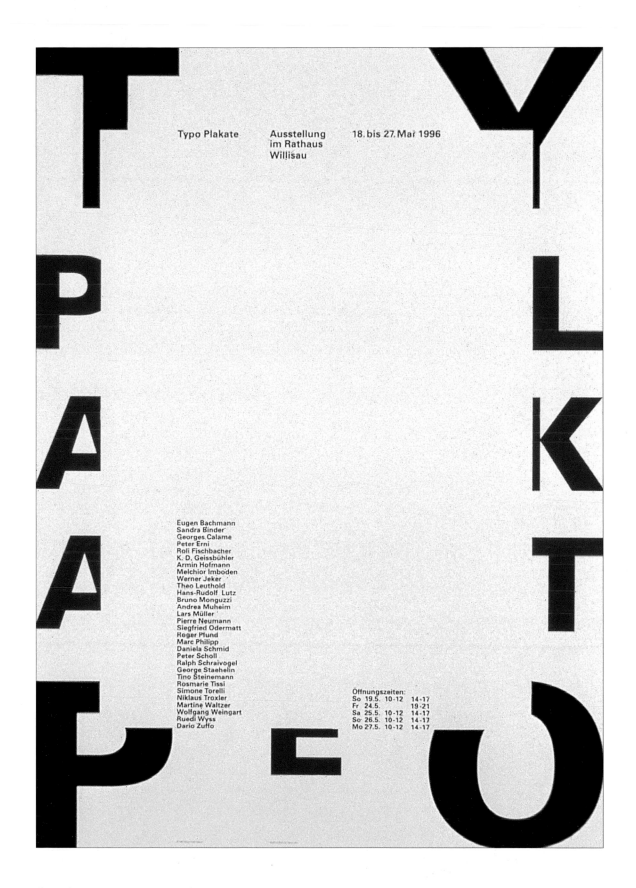

Typo Plakate   Ausstellung   18. bis 27. Mai 1996
im Rathaus
Willisau

Eugen Bachmann
Sandra Binder
Georges Calame
Peter Erni
Rolf Fischbacher
K. D. Geissbühler
Armin Hofmann
Melchior Imboden
Werner Jeker
Theo Leuthold
Hans-Rudolf Lutz
Bruno Monguzzi
Andrea Muheim
Lars Müller
Pierre Neumann
Siegfried Odermatt
Roger Pfund
Marc Philipp
Daniela Schmid
Peter Scholl
Ralph Schraivogel
George Staehelin
Tino Steinemann
Rosmarie Tissi
Simone Torelli
Niklaus Troxler
Martine Waltzer
Wolfgang Weingart
Ruedi Wyss
Dario Zuffo

Öffnungszeiten:
So 19.5. 10-12 14-17
Fr   24.5.   19-21
Sa 25.5. 10-12 14-17
So 26.5. 10-12 14-17
Mo 27.5. 10-12 14-17

(this page)
Design Firm: Niklaus Troxler Design
Creative Director, Designer,
Illustrator: Niklaus Troxler
Printer: Boesch Siebdruck
Client: Rathansbühne

(this spread)
Design Firm: Kan & Lau
Design Consultants
Creative Director, Designer:

Freeman Lau Siu Hong
Photographer, this page: C.K. Wong
Client: Hong Kong Designers
Association

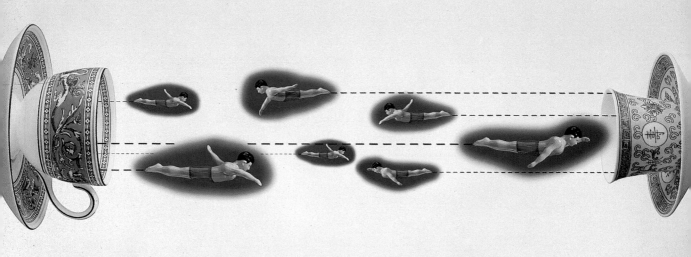

Seven Graphic Designers from Hong Kong 21 – 31 May 1996 Paper Point, 53/54, Long Acre, Covent Garden, London

Poster Designed by Freeman Lau | Printed on Conqueror CX22 from Wiggins Teape (Hong Kong) Limited

Denke
für die
a
schöne
Nacht

Deine
Utopie

(preceding page, this page)
Student: Thomas Bieling
Instructor: Uwe Loesch
School: Bergische
Universität Wuppertal
Student poster designs

Kommentare zur
Gesellschaft
**100 Jahre
Bertolt Brecht**

software

(page 256)
Design Firm: Cahan and Associates
Creative Director, Writer: Bill Cahan
Art Directors: Bill Cahan,
Dennis Scheyer
Designer: Craig Bailey
Client: Scheyer/SF
Mill Valley Film Festival Poster

Creative Directors Art Directors Designers

Photographers Illustrators

Copywriters

Design Firms

Clients

Order Graphis on the Web from anywhere in the world: www.graphis.com

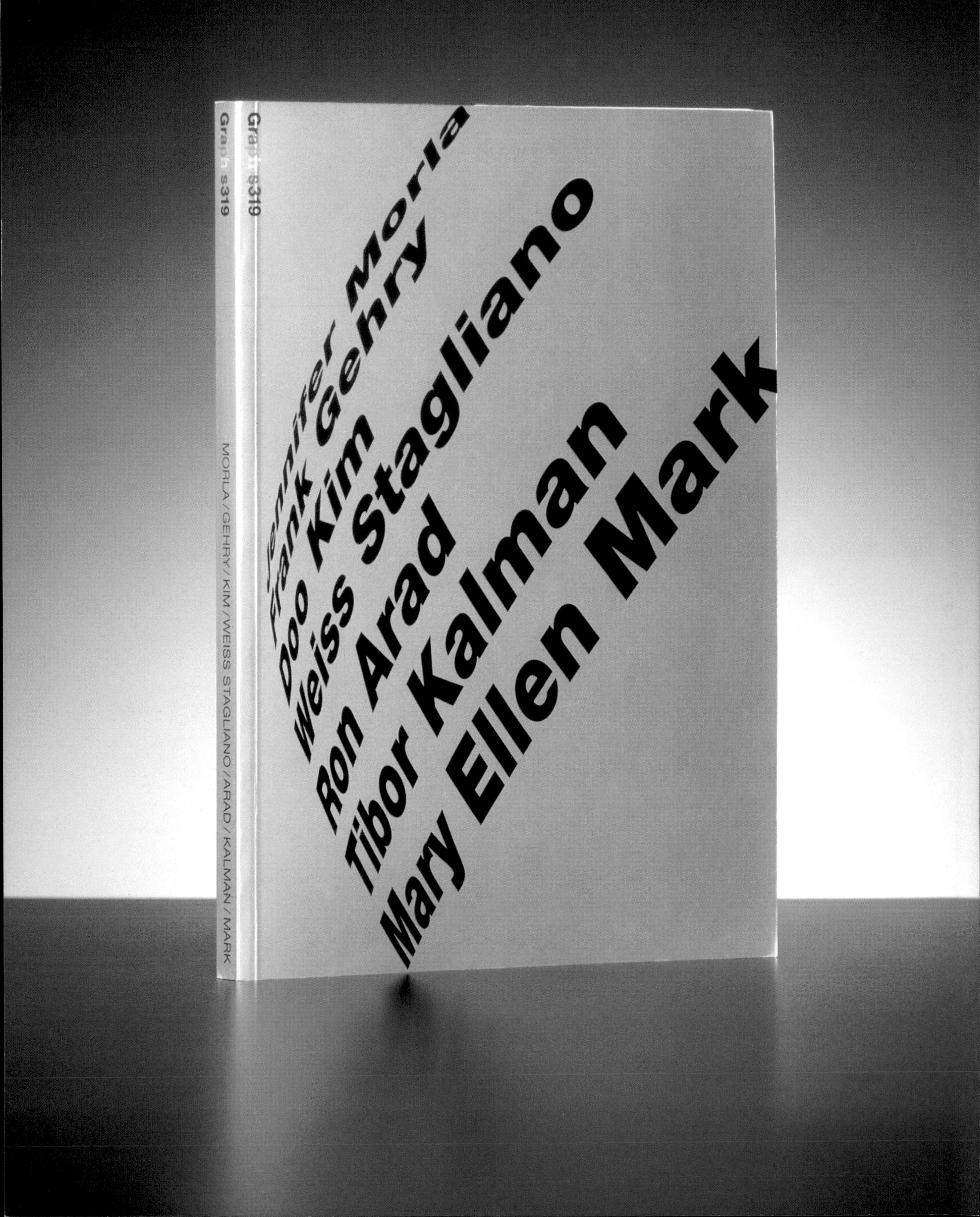
Graphis 319
MORLA / GEHRY / KIM / WEISS STAGLIANO / ARAD / KALMAN / MARK
Graphis 319
Jennifer Morla
Frank Gehry
Doo Kim
Weiss Stagliano
Ron Arad
Tibor Kalman
Mary Ellen Mark

Subscribe to our
Magazine and save
40% on all Books!

GRAPHIS
Letterhead 4

DesignAnnual1999

GRAPHIS
Annual Reports 6

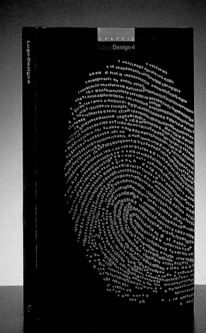
Brochures3

GRAPHIS
Corporate Identity 3

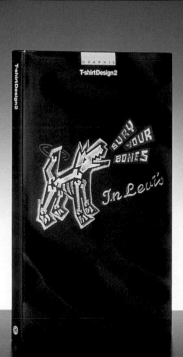
GRAPHIS
Book Design 2

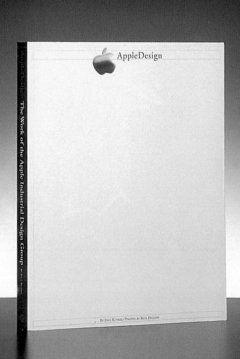
GRAPHIS
Logo Design 4

AppleDesign
The Work of the Apple Industrial Design Group

GRAPHIS
T-shirtDesign2

Order Form

We're introducing a great way to reward Graphis magazine readers: If you subscribe to Graphis, you'll qualify for a 40% discount on our books. If you subscribe and place a Standing Order, you'll get a 50% discount on our books. A Standing Order means we'll reserve your selected Graphis Annual or Series title(s) at press, and ship it to you at 50% discount. With a Standing Order for Design Annual 1999, for example, you'll receive this title at half off, and each coming year, we'll send you the newest Design Annual at this low price — an ideal way for the professional to keep informed, year after year. In addition to the titles here, we carry books in all communication disciplines, so call if there's another title we can get for you. Thank you for supporting Graphis.

Book title	Order No.	Retail	40% off Discount	standing order 50% off	Quantity	Totals
Advertising Annual 1999	1500	☐ $70.00	☐ $42.00	☐ $35.00		
Annual Reports 6 (s)	1550	☐ $70.00	☐ $42.00	☐ $35.00		
Apple Design	1259	☐ $45.00	☐ $27.00	N/A		
Black & White Blues	4710	☐ $40.00	☐ $24.00	N/A		
Book Design 2 (s)	1453	☐ $70.00	☐ $42.00	☐ $35.00		
Brochures 3 (s)	1496	☐ $70.00	☐ $42.00	☐ $35.00		
Corporate Identity 3 (s)	1437	☐ $70.00	☐ $42.00	☐ $35.00		
Design Annual 1999	1488	☐ $70.00	☐ $42.00	☐ $35.00		
Digital Photo 1 (s)	1593	☐ $70.00	☐ $42.00	☐ $35.00		
Ferenc Berko	1445	☐ $60.00	☐ $36.00	N/A		
Information Architects	1380	☐ $35.00	☐ $21.00	N/A		
Interactive Design 1 (s)	1631	☐ $70.00	☐ $42.00	☐ $35.00		
Letterhead 4 (s)	1577	☐ $70.00	☐ $42.00	☐ $35.00		
Logo Design 4 (s)	1585	☐ $60.00	☐ $36.00	☐ $30.00		
New Talent Design Annual 1999	1607	☐ $60.00	☐ $36.00	☐ $30.00		
Nudes 1	212	☐ $50.00	☐ $30.00	N/A		
Passion & Line	1372	☐ $50.00	☐ $30.00	N/A		
Photo Annual 1998	1461	☐ $70.00	☐ $42.00	☐ $35.00		
Pool Light	1470	☐ $70.00	☐ $42.00	N/A		
Poster Design Annual 1999	1623	☐ $70.00	☐ $42.00	☐ $35.00		
Product Design 2 (s)	1330	☐ $70.00	☐ $42.00	☐ $35.00		
Promotion Design 1 (s)	1615	☐ $70.00	☐ $42.00	☐ $35.00		
T-Shirt Design 2 (s)	1402	☐ $60.00	☐ $36.00	☐ $30.00		
Typography 2	1267	☐ $70.00	☐ $42.00	☐ $35.00		
Walter Iooss	1569	☐ $60.00	☐ $36.00	N/A		
World Trademarks	1070	☐ $250.00	☐ $150.00	N/A		

Shipping & handling per book, US $7.00, Canada $15.00, International $20.00.

New York State shipments add 8.25% tax.

Standing Orders I understand I am committing to the selected annuals and/or series and will be automatically charged for each new volume in forthcoming years, at 50% off. I must call and cancel my order when I am no longer interested in purchasing the book. (To honor your standing order discount you must sign below.)

Signature _____ Date _____

Graphis magazine					
	☐ One year subscription	USA $90	Canada $125	Int'l $125	
	☐ Two year subscription	USA $165	Canada $235	Int'l $235	
	☐ One year student*	USA $65	Canada $90	Int'l $90	
	☐ Single or Back Issues (per)	USA $24	Canada $28	Int'l $28	

*All students must mail a copy of student ID along with the order form.   **(s)** = series (published every 2-4 years)

Name	☐ American Express ☐ Visa ☐ Mastercard ☐ Check
Company	
Address	Card #
City State Zip	Expiration
Daytime phone	Card holder's signature

Send this order form (or copy) and make check payable to Graphis Inc. For even faster turn-around service, or if you have any questions about subscribing, call us at the following numbers: in the US (800) 209. 4234; outside the US (212) 532. 9387 ext. 242 or 241; fax (212) 696. 4242. Mailing address: Graphis, 141 Lexington Avenue, New York, New York 10016-8193. Order Graphis on the Web from anywhere in the world: <www.graphis.com>.

Advertising Annual1999

Design Annual1999

Poster Annual1998

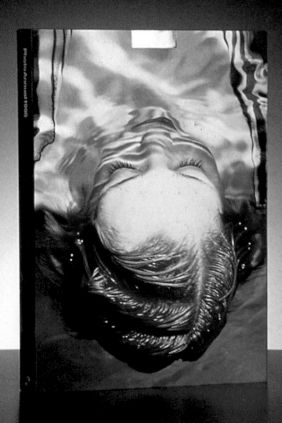

Graphis Books Call For Entry

If you would like us to put you on our Call for Entries mailing list for any of our books, please fill out the form and check off the specific books of which you would like to be a part. We now consolidate our mailings twice a year for our spring and fall books. If information is needed on specific deadlines for any of our books, please consult our website: www.graphis.com.

Graphic Design Books	☐ Poster Annual	**Photography Books**	**Student Books**
☐ Advertising Annual	☐ Products by Design	☐ Digital Photo (Professional)	☐ Advertising Annual
☐ Annual Reports	☐ Letterhead	☐ Human Cond. (Photojournalism)	☐ Design Annual
☐ Book Design	☐ Logo Design	☐ New Talent (Amateur)	☐ Photo Annual (Professional)
☐ Brochure	☐ Music CD	☐ Nudes (Professional)	☐ Products by Design
☐ Corporate Identity	☐ New Media	☐ Nudes (Fine Art)	☐ **All the Books**
☐ Design Annual	☐ Packaging	☐ Photo Annual (Professional)	☐ All Design Books only
☐ Digital Fonts	☐ Paper Promotions	☐ Photography (Fine Art)	☐ All Photo Books only
☐ Diagrams	☐ Typography		☐ All Student Books only

First Name: _____ Last Name: _____

Company: _____

Telephone: _____ Fax: _____

Mailing Address: _____ City: _____

State, Country: _____ Zip: _____

Mail form or copy to: Graphis, Call for Entries, 141 Lexington Ave., New York, New York 10016–8139, USA, or fax to (212) 213. 3229.

20th Anniversary
Mill Valley Film Festival

October 2-12, 1997
Sequoia & Lark Theatres